◆ESCAPE◆
FROM THE
KILLING FIELDS

·ESCAPE·
FROM THE
KILLING FIELDS

One Girl Who Survived The Cambodian Holocaust

NANCY MOYER

ZondervanPublishingHouse
Grand Rapids, Michigan

A Division of HarperCollins*Publishers*

Escape from the Killing Fields
One Girl Who Survived the Cambodian Holocaust
Copyright © 1991 by Nancy Moyer & Associates

Zondervan Books is an imprint of
The Zondervan Publishing House
1415 Lake Drive, S.E.
Grand Rapids, Michigan 49506

Library of Congress Cataloging-in-Publication Data:

Moyer, Nancy (Nancy Kay), 1942–
   Escape from the killing fields : one girl who survived the
Cambodian holocaust / by Nancy Moyer.
     p. cm.
   ISBN 0-310-53891-2 (paper)
   1. Lorn, Ly. 2. Cambodia—Politics and government. 3. Political
atrocities—Cambodia. 4. Refugees, Political—Cambodia—Biography.
5. Refugees, Political—United States—Biography. I. Title
DS554.83.L67M69   1990
959.604′092—dc20
   [B]   91–2184
                                                         CIP

Edited by Mary McCormick
Designed by Kim Koning

Printed in the United States of America

91 92 93 94 95 / CH / 5 4 3 2 1

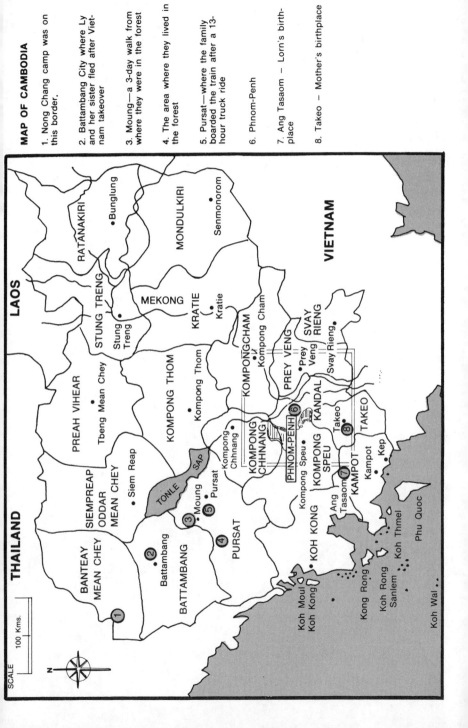

MAP OF CAMBODIA

1. Nong Chang camp was on this border.

2. Battambang City where Ly and her sister fled after Vietnam takeover

3. Moung—a 3-day walk from where they were in the forest

4. The area where they lived in the forest

5. Pursat—where the family boarded the train after a 13-hour truck ride

6. Phnom-Penh

7. Ang Tasaom – Lorn's birthplace

8. Takeo – Mother's birthplace

To the family of **Minh Thien Voan**, a courageous man who did not survive the genocide of the Pol Pot forces

and

to **Ly Lorn**, with whom I spent untold hours, who so willingly gave of herself, sharing painful memories because she understood the value of sharing these experiences

With thanks to . . .

* **Joyce Farrell**, a new friend, who believed in the story and helped to get it published, and **Mary McCormick**, the editor at Zondervan whose expertise helped me in this process
* **Lindsey Nicholls**, World Vision Director of Operations in the early '80s and Assistant to Dr. Pene Key, head doctor in the medical program
* **Dr. Marv Raley**, who also worked in the hospital—and with his wife, **Judy**, gave me helpful insights, as did
* **Carl Harris**, Associate Director of World Vision Cambodia with Minh Thien Voan
* longtime friend, **Bryan Truman**, who shared his expertise by writing the epilogue
* A number of friends, including former president of World Vision, **Dr. Stan Mooneyham**, who shared editorial ideas as well as encouragement
* Other World Vision colleagues **Ed Gruman, Norval Hadley,** and **Molly Davis-Scott,** all of whom gave me valuable editorial insights
* **Graeme Irvine**, president of World Vision International, whose assistant I am—for allowing me time to work final editing into a very busy schedule
* **My sister Ruth** and **brother Fred** who have helped me understand the value of close family relationships

* **Dorothy** and **Stewart Moyer,** my parents, whose life of love and acceptance shared with me was the basis for understanding and writing about Lorn and her precious family. My father has gone to heaven, but my mother continues to model the love that binds a family together and gives strength to the needy—whoever they are. I thank God for the gift of my family.

ក្រុម គ្រួសារ is the Cambodian word for *family*.

Contents

Cast of Characters

Ly Lorn—Main subject of the story. She was twenty-one years of age when the Khmer Rouge took over the Cambodian Government in April 1975. She was twenty-five when she escaped from Cambodia into Thailand.

Lorn's Family

Mother—Lorn's mother
Father—Lorn's father
Grandmother—Father's mother
Nan—Lorn's older sister, 23 in 1975
Meng—Nan's husband
Phanny—Lorn's younger sister, 14 in 1975
Hy—the oldest of Lorn's brothers, 17 in 1975
Heng—the second brother, 11 in 1975
Peo—the third brother, 7 in 1975
Houng—the fourth brother, 6 in 1975
Tak—the baby brother, 4 in 1975
Mouy Xea—Nan's baby, born in 1975

CAST OF CHARACTERS

Friends

Ruth Patterson—taught Bible classes in English

Dr. Pene Key—a friend of Ruth's and Director of the World Vision medical program

Isabel Broad—a nurse from Australia who worked for World Vision

Lorn is third from left (1973–74)

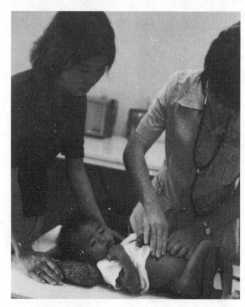

Lorn helps one of the doctors care for a baby (1974)

Foreword

Reading Ly Lorn's story is, for me, like going back into another lifetime. Her country of Cambodia has figured so largely in my own life since 1968 that I seem to have an intimate relationship with every story, every town, and many of the people in Nancy Moyer's book.

Through tears I have watched Cambodia go through the hell of war, the death throes of its national genocide, and the struggle for resurrection.

Lorn's story is that of her own personal holocaust. She was in the "killing fields" when the murderous Pol Pot presided over the death of between one and two million Cambodians, some of whom were her own family. By God's grace, she survived and has found a new life.

The country itself started to return to life when the Khmer Rouge were overthrown in 1979, but without international recognition, the road back from the dead has been one slow inch after another. Jungle warfare has continued, education can be restored only one classroom at a time, health services are still rudimentary, and food production is still below the minimum needed for survival.

In the meantime, the national psyche is slowly healing. Virtually every adult alive in Cambodia today has a story to tell of unbearable suffering under Pol Pot, a story much like Lorn's.

When the killing fields had finally received the last drop of Cambodian blood and the world learned the truth, everyone had a compulsion to tell his or her story. The need was not only for personal remembrances, but so that the world would know and never forget. I listened to countless agonies relived until it seemed I could hear no more, but I had to keep on listening because the people had to keep on telling them.

Genocide on a national scale called for nothing less than a catharsis of the same magnitude. The reason I know that healing is taking place is that now there is less need for the people to talk about the past.

Today a new generation of Cambodians has been born. They will remember the years of Lorn's suffering, for their parents will not allow them to forget. But what about the next generation? Or the one after that?

And what about the rest of the world whose memory is so short and whose concerns are eclipsed so easily? *Lorn's story is for us today and for them tomorrow.*

Its message for all is, "**Never again! Never again!**" So help us God.

—Stan Mooneyham
(Former president of World Vision)

Preface

My introduction to Cambodia was in 1970 when the organization for which I work, World Vision International, received an urgent request for assistance from the Cambodian Red Cross. We were able to respond quickly, meeting some of the basic needs of many of the Cambodian people. The war had forced them away from the countryside and into the cities. **They were refugees in their own country.** From that small but significant beginning, World Vision built a major program in Cambodia, with a strong medical component. A hospital was eventually built that is once again being used as a place of comfort and healing.

In 1970 I was working for World Vision's president, Dr. Stan Mooneyham. Almost daily, my work brought me into contact with our Cambodian colleagues. The opportunities to help the people grew until the Khmer Rouge (Red Cambodian) forces finally overthrew the government of the Republic of Cambodia on April 17, 1975.

I had felt love from afar for the Cambodian people and will never forget the warmth and generosity with which I was received when I visited in March 1973. The country was beautiful, but it was being raped and abused.

Evidence of war was all around. I had never before

been in a refugee camp. I had never seen people without homes and having to live in squalid, unsanitary conditions—never before looked into the eyes of people who were starving to death—never seen little children whose parents had no way to feed them. The impact was profound. I returned to America with a greater love for these people, who, because of an insane war, had been reduced from self-sufficient citizens to refugees.

The happiest memory of my visit to Phnom Penh was meeting Minh Thien Voan, the Deputy Director of World Vision's ministry in Cambodia. For several days I watched him at work. I saw how one person, willing to give himself to the task of helping hurting people, could make a difference. I was encouraged. There was hope. My visit was short, but before I left, my friendship with Voan and his wife, Thery, was firmly established. I had a Cambodian family and left a part of my heart with them.

As the world watched, the war became more destructive. Just before the Khmer Rouge leader, Pol Pot, came into power in 1975, Voan sent his family to America. Thery bravely came with the children, Sophie, Paul, and Dannielle. They captured my heart as they became a major part of my life. Voan stayed in Cambodia, feeling that his duty was to stay a while longer with the suffering people in his country. He didn't know that the last flight had gone. Later we heard that Voan was killed by a blow to the back of his neck. It happened April 17, 1975—the day the Khmer Rouge overtook the country.

A part of my reason for writing this book is my love for Voan and his family. Another reason, of course, is my love for Lorn, the heroine of this book. For most of us, tragedy is a singular experience that comes and passes.

PREFACE

For Ly Lorn, tragedy peaked for four, long, hard years. It was nearly overpowering.

There have been many other heroes—people who either had their lives taken by the Khmer Rouge, or because of Khmer Rouge brutality were forced to leave their homes and enter a country filled with strange new customs, people, and a difficult-to-learn language. They have no hope of ever returning to the comfort and familiarity of their homeland.

Most of us have grown up in countries with a legacy of hospitality toward people without a country, but not many of us as individuals have accepted into our hearts one or more of these people we call refugees. We haven't worked very hard at understanding them or allowed them to know us well enough to understand us. These are a gentle people—they will not force themselves upon us.

It's important for us to feel some of the terror of the refugee. Perhaps then we will understand how to make it easier for them to be comfortable in our country. These are our neighbors. We have been commanded—and blessed with the privilege—to love them and to ease their pain of uncertainty and loneliness. As Christians, we must remember Christ's words, "Inasmuch as ye have done it unto one of the least of these my brethren, ye have done it unto me" (Matt. 26:40).

No one person can change the apathy we see all around us, but we **can** control the infiltration into our own hearts and minds of a complacent attitude toward the desperate needs of other human beings. *Escape from the Killing Fields* is the true story of the near-annihilation of an entire group of people and their country. Because it happened so far away, we tend to think that it's not our concern. I hope this story will help many to understand that it **is** our concern. We **must** care. I hope, too, that it will help us appreciate the value of our freedom.

It is estimated that nearly two million died between 1975 and 1979 under the cruel hand of the Khmer Rouge. This is not an attempt to understand the political issues, but it does present the opportunity to share in the agony and the ecstasy of one young woman.

My heart was filled with these thoughts the day I met Lorn and began hearing her tell of her experiences. I was challenged with the opportunity to tell her story, and I could not turn it down. She is a beautiful person who, in God's strength, has emerged without bitterness from four terror-filled years of living under the dominance of the Khmer Rouge regime when people all around her were dying.

Knowing Ly Lorn has been a life-changing experience. I've been humbled and chastened as well as encouraged, challenged, and blessed. I pray that God will use Lorn's story to touch your life in a similarly beneficial way.

I am reminded of the tribute Malcolm Muggeridge paid Mother Teresa, and I believe that the life and testimony of Ly Lorn is also "something beautiful for God."

—Nancy Moyer

A NOTE FROM LY LORN

My name is Lorn. For the first twenty-five years of my life, I lived in Cambodia. Most of these were filled with happiness and security. I lived with my wonderful family and enjoyed the love and peaceful life that is so important to children.

The opportunity to openly express ourselves was something we did not have during the last five years I lived in Cambodia. That was such a sad time that I try not to remember it. Because I don't think most people would ever believe it, I think it's important to tell you the story of what happened to me during the years under the Khmer Rouge and how I survived. As you read, I hope you will begin to better understand my people. Please pray especially for those who still live in Cambodia. They continue to live under great pressure and difficulty.

1

My City Dies

*As I walked through the home we had
enjoyed so much, I looked longingly at
each room. In my heart I knew I would
never see them again.*

*. . . The memories I had to leave behind
were like friends, but I tearfully tore
myself away as Father called, "Lorn, we
must go! Hurry! Quickly!"*

The story begins on a very frightening night in 1975. I was twenty-one years old, the second of eight children.

That hot, humid night of April 16, 1975, thunderous, exploding sounds of rockets and shells filled the air and continued unendingly into the next day. As my family and I prepared for the long night hours, Father assigned us to sleep in three different rooms so that if a rocket hit our house, perhaps only part of our family would die. Father took my brothers, Heng and Tak, with him into one room. My oldest brother, Hy, took our little brothers Houng and Peo with him into another room. Mother, my sister Phanny, and my sister Nan with her 12-day-old baby boy, and I went in the third bedroom. We lay under pieces of furniture with many blankets over us in the hope of being protected if our house was hit.

The night sky was bright from the explosions and fires rampant in the city. I snuggled close to Phanny, trying not to think about what Phnom Penh would be like after these days of horrible war—or what would happen to all of us who called it home. But I knew we would have to face it soon.

When it was finally time to get up on Thursday morning, April 17, I was hesitant to leave the family and go to work. My brother Hy and I worked at one of the clinics run by World Vision, an international Christian relief organization. Although I knew that the 48-hour curfew the government had declared on the morning of April 16 was not over, some of our neighbors had gone

Lorn with a member of the World Vision Board of Directors, Rev. John Rymer, Dean of Anglican Church, Auckland, New Zeeland (1974)

out and come back safely. Hy convinced me by saying, "We have not been to the clinic for three days because of the Cambodian New Year and the curfew. There must be many refugees and soldiers who need our help." If we were needed, of course we must go.

With Mother's "Please be careful!" ringing in our ears, we set off on Hy's motorbike toward the clinic.

It did not take us long to travel the five kilometers. As we approached, I was surprised to see that there were no lines of refugees waiting. Usually at least five hundred would have gathered, anxious for the medicine, vitamins, and other kinds of help we could give. Even with the curfew, we thought some would be there. Hy and I talked of waiting to see if people would come, although even if they did, we were helpless. The clinic was locked and no doctors were there to take charge. After a quick discussion—with the rockets hitting around us—Hy and I decided that before returning home we would stop at the clinic in the village, where several of the World Vision medical staff lived.

This must have been a more secure area, because there were people all around. When we drove into the village center, Dr. SokNan, one of the World Vision doctors, welcomed us, asking that we first put on smocks identifying us as part of the medical team, and then get to work.

The people suffered greatly. For months they had been coming to us with typhus, malaria, infections, severe malnutrition, and tuberculosis. This day, victims of rocket and gunshot wounds were added to the crowd. We worked feverishly with the others for more than two hours, giving medicine, cleaning wounds, helping the doctors, and trying to encourage the hurting, frightened people.

About 9:30 A.M. I had a strong intuition that Hy and I should return home. As we raced through the city streets, we had to swerve often to dodge the volley of shells falling all around us. As I prayed for God's protection from the dangers, it surprised me when I heard a voice coming out of the sky—over a loud speaker, I soon realized. It was a Communist leader shouting, "The war is ended! The war is ended!" Soldiers, wearing black and carrying white flags, came from every direction. Now rockets were flying like fireworks, primarily to get people's attention.

The street was crowded with people wearing mostly black uniforms. I recognized some of Lon Nol's people, who had taken off their army uniforms and come into the streets in civilian clothes to greet the new rulers. Everyone was happily hugging and kissing each other. Soon there was a chorus of voices, "The war is over!" ... There would be peace again.

Hy and I didn't know what to think of all this, but it made him drive faster toward our home and family. As we rushed into the house, there was an almost deathly, eerie silence. Frightened, we ran through the house, calling "Mother!—Father!" and found them hiding in a back room with our brothers and sisters. Mother sobbed as she told of the horror they had experienced just ten minutes earlier.

Two large Khmer Rouge soldiers, carrying guns and dressed in the same black uniforms we had seen on the streets, had pounded at our door. When Mother opened it, they pushed past her into the house, shouting that the family must evacuate. They said, "Do not pack very many things. You will be back home in a few days. Above all, the city must be empty by nightfall because the Americans are going to bomb us." Mother's immediate fear had been that Hy and I might not return before the family was forced to leave. Because we were all together, we momentarily forgot the immediate danger.

Reality set in very soon as our family of eleven huddled together, fearful that a passing soldier might see or hear us. We had to develop a strategy. Part of it required finding our relatives who lived in other parts of the city. My grandmother, aunt, and her family of seven lived next door.

The houses were so close together that Father had been able to talk to them from our back porch. Taking charge, he said, "Stay in the house until I give the signal, and we will leave together as one family." He was hoping we could wait a while to see if our other relatives would come by our house on their way out of town. Grandmother was especially worried about one of her daughters who was a widow and lived alone because her children were married. We must make contact with her. Everything would be all right if we were together.

Decisions had to be made. As we told the family what we had seen on the streets, Father said, "I don't trust the soldiers. I don't believe their promise that we are only leaving the city for a few days while the new leadership defends us against American bombings." We decided we would take more with us than the soldiers had suggested, so we were each assigned something to carry.

We did not have the luxury of contemplating for very long on what to take. Time was valuable. Father and Hy stayed with the little ones, and Nan kept the baby content. Mother, Phanny, and I crept through the house collecting the most valuable items. We took the gold Father had saved, as well as food, rice, some blankets, clothing, and medicine for my sister Nan and her baby.

Mother did not have very much good jewelry, but there was one special necklace that Father's mother had given her on their wedding day. She took that, and I slipped into my pocket a necklace I had bought with some of the money I had earned working at World Vision. I also took the New Testament that my friend Ruth Patterson had given me, and a photograph of Isabel Broad—the nurse I worked most with at the clinic. According to our age, Father gave us each some Cambodian money to use if we became separated. I was given 20,000 riels, and put it inside my underclothing for safe keeping.

The most important thing to take was food. Mother said, "If we have enough good food we can survive anything," so she packed everything possible. We had a few baskets that we could fill, but everything else had to be tied into bundles that we carried on our heads.

As I walked through the home we had enjoyed so much, I looked longingly at each room. In my heart I knew I would never see them again. Standing in the door of the living room, I couldn't help notice the lovely furniture we had finally been able to buy for Mother, and the portable television. How the little boys had loved that! I wished that we had been able to enjoy these things for longer than just a few months. Moving through the bedrooms, I saw on the walls special photographs and other things that each of us treasured. Father's cautionary "Don't take anything we don't need" kept me from putting them into my bag.

When I reached the room that Nan, Phanny, and I shared, I went to look at myself in the long mirror and thought about the first time I had experimented with makeup in front of it. At age twenty-one I loved being a girl and had found that a little lipstick, mascara, and eyeshadow made me feel even more feminine.

Forgetting Father's caution, I decided I had room for some of my favorite perfumes and makeup. I would have to carry these things in addition to the food Father had already assigned to me, but I wanted them enough to do it. I also had to decide how many pieces of clothing to take. Like most girls, I overpacked for the occasion, but then I didn't really know the occasion.

I heard pounding at our front door and ran to see

Father opening it. Again I saw soldiers in black uniforms. I would see many of them in the months ahead but never liked one of them. There was a surliness about those men that instinctively caused me to feel both fear and resentment. They had their hands on their guns as if ready to use them while they repeated their orders, savagely shouting, "We will shoot you without a question if we see you in this house again. You must leave at once."

My father's glance seemed to say, "The time is now, dear children."

It was nearly 5:00 P.M. I felt desperate and knew these were my last moments in our home. I ran back to my room. On the floor was a favorite pair of high-heeled shoes. I grabbed them, putting them into an already overflowing basket of clothing. By taking the shoes I felt that I was taking something far more meaningful—the spirit and happy memories of that room and our home. The memories I had to leave behind were like friends, but I tearfully tore myself away as Father called, "Lorn, we must go! Hurry! Quickly!"

Father had gathered my grandmother, aunt, and her family, so there were twenty of us who walked down our small street that day. It didn't even have a name, but when we got to the corner where the 18th of March Street crossed it, I stopped and turned around to look at our home again. The huge, flowering tree in front was in full bloom, and our little house stood there proudly as if to say, *I will be here when you return.*

With tears in my eyes I turned the corner with my loved ones, praying we would somehow meet my widowed aunt and the other relatives we loved so much—but we never saw their faces again.

Some of our neighbors were walking near us. We could only hurriedly ask where they were planning to go. The soldiers had told us to walk out of the city, heading toward the birthplace of one of our elders. Many of the residents of Phnom Penh were country people who had come to the city in the last five or six years, when the war had become dangerous in their provinces. Now, the Khmer Rouge reasoned, we should go back to the area from which we had come.

"Pick a route that will get you out of the city as quickly as possible," the soldiers ordered, so we began walking south toward Takeo, where my mother and her sister were born. Because we were not allowed to take our car or bicycles, even the little ones had to walk.

As we became part of the flood of people near the Olympic Stadium, we saw that some had risked taking their cars, filling them with possessions and pushing them through the crowd. Sometimes sick or old people were riding inside. Father wondered if we should have tried doing that, but we could not go back now. Soldiers walked through the streets, shooting their guns into the air to frighten the people and make them walk faster.

But that was impossible. The crush of people moving together at an incredibly slow pace was intense and never-ending. Most people were on foot and, like my family, trying to carry as many things as possible. We could only walk a few steps before having to stop. Sometimes we would have to just stand still for several minutes, which gave us plenty of time to look around.

Many buildings in our beautiful city had been blown up or gutted out by the rockets and fires. The bad smell was overwhelming. Father explained, "That is the smell of death. I think many people have died in those buildings and their bodies have never been taken away." That was the first time I experienced the stomach-turning smell of death.

Even though it was late afternoon, it was still extremely hot. We were so dazed at the scene around us that we hardly noticed the weather. Children were crying—some were lost and screaming in vain for a familiar face. Many adults were crying out names, searching for their little ones or for other family members.

Because people were pushing at us so constantly, it took all of our concentration to be sure that the twenty of us stayed together. It was hard even to make a conversation. It was especially important that none of the little ones lagged behind in the crowd, or they would have been forever lost to us.

As we shuffled slowly along National Road #2, each of us was lost in our own thoughts and fears. As one mile stretched into several miles, we became more and more appalled at the cruelties around us. I could not believe it when I saw hospitalized patients being carried or dragged along by family members. I remember saying to Hy, "These must be patients from the Russian-built hospital. But why? Where can the soldiers expect them to go?"

Some were lying on beds pushed by loved ones, with plasma and glucose bottles bumping alongside. There were mothers in the midst of giving birth, and patients left in the middle of surgery by doctors and nurses who had to think of their own welfare—and many died right there as we watched helplessly.

We were a mass of humanity desperate to stay together as a family, but with no idea of what the future held for us, or even what was happening to us at that moment. As we walked, there were pitiful people all around. I remember seeing one old man alone and not carrying anything, who looked so sad and lonely in the middle of that crowd of people. I wondered where his family was.

Many families had been separated. One man told my father, "I was at work in the south part of town when they forced us to evacuate this way. I was not allowed a chance to communicate with my wife and children, who were at home in the northern part of the city. Now, I'm sure they are some place looking for me; but even if I knew where, it would not be possible to walk against this crowd of people to go a different direction in the hope of finding them." I breathed a "Thank you, Lord, for my family and for letting us be together. Please help us be strong."

The rebel Khmer Rouge (Red Cambodian) forces had moved into the city quietly but effectively with a highly organized plan set up to evacuate our city of more than three million residents. Some of these people were refugees who had recently fled to our city, hoping for safety and security.

We had no way of knowing that part of the plan of these soldiers and their leaders was to gain complete control of our entire civilization. Moving three million people out of a city in such a short period of time is an amazing feat. The fact that it was possible and happening in cities all over our country proved that the gentle Cambodian people were anxious to live in peace at any cost—to *bend with the breeze, like bamboo,* as the Khmer saying goes.

Even the leadership in the now-defeated Khmer

Republic was too naïve to believe they would not be able to agree with other Khmers—their own countrymen. Surely there was room in the new regime for everyone! The genocide that was to take place was beyond the comprehension of every true Cambodian, thus we did not at once recognize its true identity when it boldly began to show its ugly face.

The crowded roads made it very dangerous to walk at night. "I'm afraid we might lose someone in the crowd because this is the time of the month when the moon is not very bright," Father said. It would be easier in a week or so when the moon was more full. About 8:00 P.M. the first night we stopped to rest and eat at a lovely piece of farmland we had found outside the city limits.

Our bed was the ground with a blanket—the sky our roof. We were all thankful it did not rain that night. There were enough problems without that.

As we trudged on, one day moved into the next. We walked slowly by villages that had been destroyed, but we were afraid to approach them because some of the soldiers might still be in the area. I especially remember seeing the little town of Demroka, and feeling sad to see the bombed-out buildings. "Remember when we used to come here?" I said to Mother. "It was always so lovely." "Many of the buildings are made of stone, so perhaps the soldiers used the town as a fortress," Father thought aloud. The streets were heavily littered with things taken from homes and stores; television sets, appliances, and cars that had been destroyed. It was difficult for us to understand the destruction of such expensive items. Because the highway went through the town, we again experienced the heavy stench of death.

It didn't take us many days to realize how fortunate

we were that Father had been wise enough to insist on our bringing so many essentials—especially food. We were sorry for those who had brought little or nothing because they had believed the soldiers when they said we would be back in the city within a few days.

Many died during our first few days on the road. We wished we could help them, but if we had started to do that, our supply wouldn't have lasted long. Besides, we wouldn't have helped anyone enough to make a great difference anyway. So we saved our treasured rice and food for Mother to carefully ration each day.

It was always good to hear Father say we could stop walking for a short time and sit under a tree while Mother fixed a little rice for us to eat. Before we had time to rest even a short while, the soldiers would be there to prod us on. They had no sympathy at all. If someone in the family was sick, one could not stop and sit with them. Instead, one was forced to keep on moving and leave them by themselves if they could not move.

Everyone was intensely hungry and tired. Children cried for food, and people begged the soldiers, "When can we have a little bit of food to give to our family?" They always responded with an empty promise, such as "Just a few kilometers ahead an organization has food waiting for you. You must hurry, though, to be sure the others don't get it first." That, of course, made everyone walk faster. But no matter how fast or far we walked, we never found that food.

It was common to see dead bodies by the roadside. Most had simply been too hungry or sick to take another step. Others, with their hands tied behind them, had obviously been killed. With fear, I wondered, *What could they have done to deserve this and will anyone give them a proper burial?* No one had an answer.

Seeing so many sick and dying people caused us to be concerned for ourselves, so when we did talk while walking along, it was usually about the food supply, how long it would last, and what we would do when it ran out. I overheard Father ask Mother if she thought he would be able to get work right away in order to keep us supplied with essentials. She couldn't answer because even though we were going to her home, she was not sure what the situation there would be like.

There were so many unknowns, so many things of which we were uncertain as we walked along the still-crowded highway. We didn't know how many days it would take us to walk to Takeo. After two weeks had gone by, Father assured us, "We are at least halfway there. Please stay strong." He was our leader and our motivator.

Mother looked forward to returning to her birthplace, Takeo, which was just a few kilometers from Ang Tasaom, the place where both of my sisters, four of my brothers, and I had been born. My youngest brother, Tak, was born in Phnom Penh early in 1971. I still thought of him as "the baby." We had been forced to leave Ang Tasaom in 1970 when our village was bombed. At that time we went with many other villagers to Phnom Penh to escape the effects of war that had spread throughout the countryside.

Now it made us feel good to know we were at least going to a familiar area. We knew the country was in a state of turmoil, but the dream of returning to some semblance of the peaceful, happy life of our childhood made leaving Phnom Penh less painful. I silently prayed we were heading toward safety and security.

2

Memories of Takeo

As we were walking, I heard someone around me say that the soldiers searched people and if they found anything linking them to the Western world they would kill them ... At the same time, I thought of my New Testament but could not relinquish it. That was a risk I was willing to take.

As we walked, I had hours to think. In fact, it was much more pleasant to drown in my memories than to face the realities around me.

I couldn't recall ever having been sad during my first sixteen years. Life flowed around me gently like the Mekong river that winds through the beautiful Cambodian countryside. The reason for my happiness was my family.

My parents were wonderful. Father owned a fabric store and Mother ran our household. When we left Ang Tasaom in 1970, I was sixteen. My sister Nan was eighteen, Hy was twelve, and my sister Phanny was nine. My younger brothers, Heng, Peo, and Houng were six, three, and nearly two years old, in that order. Mother was pregnant with Tak.

Growing up was a joyful experience filled with loved ones. Our extended family was almost as close as our immediate family. Father's mother was an important part of our whole life, and it was a special treat to be able to take the bus to her home. When we did not have enough money for that, we would ride our bicycles. I used to say to Mother, "I don't really care how we get there, as long as we can be with her," so Mother often allowed us to leave our chores and go.

Many of the brothers and sisters of my parents lived near our home, and I love to remember the evenings our families spent together. After the evening meal everyone would gather in front of one house. I can still feel the warmth of the night air filled with the fragrance of the trees and flowers in bloom. Mother especially liked it when the rose bushes were full. "I love to fill my home with the smell of roses and the sounds of family being together," she would say happily.

I can see the faces of my loved ones sitting in front of our house in the moonlight, laughing and talking, sharing stories, singing songs—enjoying the companionship. As children, we delighted in playing games, and sometimes our parents would watch us play what Americans call "hide-and-seek." The love of all these people so thoroughly and completely surrounded us that we felt almost as though they were our immediate family.

Having the problems of neither the rich nor the poor, we were contented and knew that our lifestyle was the best anyone could ever want to have. We were secure. We were happy.

As we walked on toward Takeo, I thought wistfully of the good times Father and I had enjoyed as we worked together in his store. He was such a good tailor, and I was proud that people came from far away to have him make their clothes. I loved being his "partner" in the store. "Always do a good job and be honest," he said. "Your customers will return and you will be happy inside yourself."

Dear *Mother*—the strength of our home and family life. She was always there when we needed her, and communicated her everlasting love in everything she did for us. She sewed our clothes, taught us to cook and to take care of our home—all with joy, but the most important thing we learned from her was the value of loving each other, no matter what else happened.

MEMORIES OF TAKEO

We lived in a beautiful country and we loved our little village of Ang Tasaom, but when the government of Prince Norodom Sihanouk gave way to that of Prime Minister Lon Nol in 1970, bombs from the American planes attempting to destroy the Communist forces in the area fell around and on our precious little province like rain.

The crashing sounds of war that had been in our ears for weeks invaded our lives, and bombs eventually fell on our home, burning it to nothing. Soon there was no town, and we were forced to leave.

Father wanted to stay in the area in the hope of returning to our land when the war became less dangerous, so we walked to his friend's farm several kilometers away and lived there for two months. When it became apparent that the war was spreading throughout the countryside, he knew the danger was not going to ease and that we could not return home.

"Our only hope," he told us sadly, "is to move to the capital city for security." We hired motorbikes and drivers for the whole family and in July 1970, began our journey to Phnom Penh.

Because of the threat of the Communist forces, the roads were unsafe. It was a several-hour ride through the forests and fields. Each kilometer was filled with heartbreak as we saw the realities of burned-out villages, bridges hit by rockets and no longer usable, dead bodies, and people like ourselves—walking or riding away from the security of a familiar place and into a bewildering, frightening future.

Returning to Takeo Province in 1975, after five years of living in Phnom Penh, was also frightening, but I wanted so much to believe that the return to the country was our answer for a new life, for happiness, for security. "Together as a family we can make it," Father often reminded me. Forcing myself back to the present and the people walking with me toward a difficult-to-anticipate life as farmers, I silently admitted that I was very afraid. *Please, God,* I prayed, *give me Your strength. Help me to help my family.*

It was the monsoon season, so when it wasn't raining, the humidity and heat were intense. If one walked in either the torrential rain or heat for long—especially with an empty stomach—one could become very ill. Nan and Grandmother were both weak, so we protected them by walking as little as possible in the sun.

At the time of month when the moon was bright, we would walk all night and stop by midday. When that was impossible, we would begin walking at first light— about 4:00 A.M., stopping to rest when the sun became intense. We would try to find a place under some trees, near water, to give us the chance to wash the mud from our bodies as well as to have water for cooking.

Often Mother would say, "If we were in Phnom Penh, I wouldn't wash clothes in this water." Now we sometimes were so thirsty that we drank it before she had time to boil it. Fortunately, Father had brought medicines that kept us from getting ill from drinking contaminated water.

We couldn't stay in one place for very long before the soldiers would come to move us on. Father always stalled as long as possible, saying, "Just a few more minutes. Let the old woman and children rest a bit." Some soldiers were more lenient than others, but most would force us to move on. Then we would walk a ways farther, stopping again when the soldiers were out of sight.

When walking with soldiers nearby, we were careful to stay very close together. If we hadn't, they might have separated us. Sometimes they would randomly motion for a few people to take a side road one way and for another group to go in the opposite direction, often breaking up a family. If this meant that some people were walking away from the village from which they had originally come, the Khmer Rouge simply reasoned that it was not possible for too many people to settle in one location. They didn't care what the people thought.

Usually the soldiers were very young men or even boys. They were unsophisticated farm people who detested city people, resenting the fact that as farmers they had always felt subservient to them. Almost none of the soldiers could read or write Khmer. Learning English and French was totally out of the question. Knowing this, one can understand how difficult it was for city people to know how to relate to these peasants who were now cruel soldiers and the people with full authority over us.

As we were walking, I heard someone around me say that the soldiers searched people and if they found anything linking them to the Western world they would kill them. I thought of my precious photograph of Isabel. I hated giving it up, but was afraid that if found, the sight of her Australian smile would endanger us all. So, I took one long last look at her face before carefully putting the photo under some leaves near a tree. At the same time, I thought of my New Testament, but could not relinquish it. That was a risk I was willing to take.

It was still very crowded as thousands of us walked

along the road. Just a few weeks before, we had all enjoyed the basic necessities of life—some had even been wealthy. Now we had nothing.

There was no difference between the rich and the poor. At first, rich men tried to use their money to buy food and win favors from the soldiers, but suddenly we learned it had no power. "In fact," Father said, "having very much money could be dangerous."

The entire monetary system had been declared worthless by the new regime. Someone told us, "The soldiers opened the bank vaults and threw the money to the wind."

"Even so," Father said, "keep what I have given to you. Someday it may be valuable again."

Whenever found, gold, watches, jewelry, and any other things of value were confiscated at checkpoints. People were usually promised that these would be returned at a later date, but of course they never were. Mother and I both dearly loved the necklaces we had brought with us, so we tried to keep them very well hidden. Thus, life became very disorganized and confusing as we lived out of our little bags and bundles. One day word was passed back to us that we were approaching a checkpoint.

I hurriedly looked for my necklace so that I could be sure it was well hidden. I couldn't find it, so that night I thoroughly searched everything and sadly realized that I had lost it somewhere along the way. Later in our journey to Takeo, Mother had a similar experience and cried when she could not find her precious necklace. She had had it for so many years and was very sad to have lost it. "At least," she said, "we did not have to give those things up to the soldiers."

For twenty days our family of twenty walked, ate, and slept together under the trees. It was very difficult. We were all hungry, tired, and dirty, and we longed for the security of a place to call home. We kept reminding each other that we were going to Mother's birthplace. She would know people there. "Now we'll have a safe, secure, and good life," Mother promised.

Finally the day came when we arrived in Takeo Province. Mother could hardly wait to see familiar faces, people she had known as a child and with whom she had grown up. At last our long walk had proven to be worthwhile. We would be happy again.

It did not take long for that dream to die. As Mother approached some of these "old friends" on behalf of us all, she began telling them of our terrible twenty-day ordeal. What a shock to us all when we realized they were not excited to see us. In fact, having been forced to become part of the Khmer Rouge, these farm people—like the soldiers—had been convinced that we were the enemy and they were openly hostile, shouting, "We hate you. You left the countryside to become rich city people, living easy while we stayed here working the fields."

As Khmer Rouge soldiers looked on, these village people said they would not be our friends, and we suddenly felt very let down and frightened. What were we to do now?

Hy, Heng, Phanny, and I were sent to the forest to get wood and bamboo to build our house. We made many trips, picking up all the pieces we could carry. I tried to make a game out of it for the others, but it was hard to make this a happy time. Some of the village people were

41

then ordered by the soldiers to help my father, brother, and uncle build our "house."

It looked like a chicken house with a thatched roof. It was small—maybe six by five feet—but it was our one-room home for the next four months. When they finished with ours, another was built for my aunt's family. There was not much room for comfort in either one. Our beds were pieces of wood filled with many splinters, but they kept us away from the bugs and the dampness of the ground. "I should have brought more blankets to keep us warm," Mother said with regret.

When it was not raining, some of us children would sleep outside in makeshift hammocks to leave more room inside for the others. There was not much to eat during these months—something we never became accustomed to. I remember special times when one of the old village people who knew Mother, would secretly give us some of the better food they received.

As city people, we received only a daily can of rice for each adult and a half-can for a child. "Your children do not work until they are twelve," the soldiers told my mother when she asked about the difference, "so they do not require much food." We really missed having salt and something besides rice and corn in our diet, and I quickly learned that it hurts to be hungry.

Too, as city people, we had never known hard, physical work, so our bodies had to make major adjustments. We arrived at the fields at 6:30 in the morning and worked straight through until 5:30 in the evening with only a one-hour rest at lunch time. My back hurt, my feet hurt, and I was hungry—all the time. It was depressing to wake up in the morning because I had nothing to look forward to and only wished I could turn and go back to sleep.

During those dark, lonely days, I first began to see in Father's eyes a helpless look that still haunts me. Sometimes I would awaken in the night to see him staring through the opening in our house that served as our door. When I would plead with him, "Please, Father, try to sleep," he always responded, "I am an old man, Daughter. You must not worry about me, because you need to sleep so you can stay strong and take care of the family." It made me sad to see him like this. He had always been our leader. Now his stomach was empty, his body weak from the unending pressure to work hard, and there was never a happy day or reason to hope that life would get better for those he loved so much.

For doing this to my father—and to all of us—I was very angry with the Khmer Rouge. I could not understand how any Cambodian could treat another Cambodian the way the soldiers treated us.

One day while working in the fields, I overheard someone whispering that "the farmers are being forced to treat all new city people as deserters." I knew the soldiers had probably been threatened with death if they helped us, but even that wasn't a good enough reason for the way we were being treated. Excuses didn't ease my family's suffering. Excuses could not return my father's love of life.

I often thought of John 3:16 and prayed, always silently, *God, I know You loved us enough to send Jesus to us. I love You, too, and pray that my family will come to love You.* Hy was the only family member who had ever listened to me when I talked about my love for Jesus. He told me that he loved Him, too, but he was not a strong Christian. The rest of my family was all Buddhist because my parents had been raised to believe very strongly in Buddha.

My most prized possession during those days was a small New Testament that was written in English. I risked my life by carrying it with me from 1975 until it was stolen with some of my clothing in 1978. Whenever I had a spare moment and was certain the Khmer Rouge were not watching or listening, I would slip it from under the waist of my skirt and read a promise, quickly explaining it to whoever of the family was around me. If caught, we would have been killed immediately, so I had to do this very carefully.

I felt a sense of urgency about this because I knew that without God's strength as their resource, the days ahead would be more difficult for these loved ones. I wanted them to know and understand what it means to be a part of God's family, to feel that "peace that passeth understanding." There was no time to say all of this without being overheard by a soldier or one of the Khmer Rouge spies, but I tried to demonstrate God's love in my actions and in everything I did for my family in the midst of the horror around us.

After four months of living in our little "chicken house," working in the fields, digging, and carrying heavy baskets of dirt to help build a canal, all with too little food, soldiers came around shouting, "All city people must meet in the field for special news."

As we sat in small groups in one corner of the field, our leader said, "The main leader has sent word that all city people are to join him in Battambang Province. He is waiting to welcome you in this rice-growing center. Now you will be able to grow enough rice to feed many people, including your own families." We didn't know the name of the "main leader," but we were anxious to join him and took great hope in the promise of security—a place to live and grow enough rice to feed our family.

We were to leave the next day, and happily went to bed that night, waiting for the time to get up so that we could begin our journey to Battambang Province, a more secure life, and the chance to eat whenever we were hungry. *Hope still existed!*

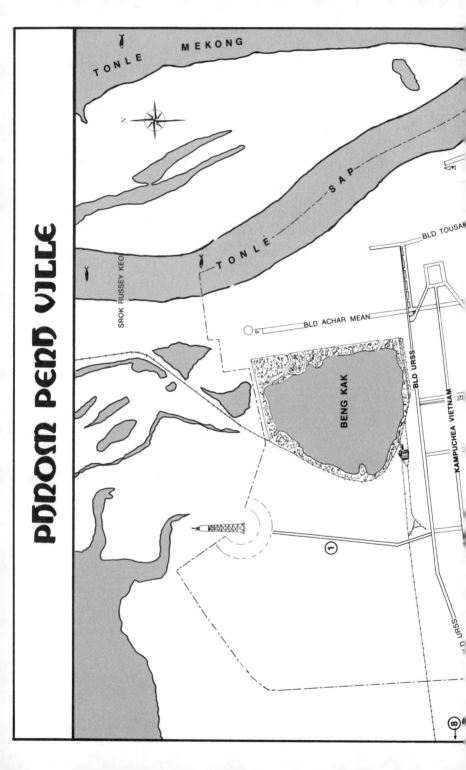

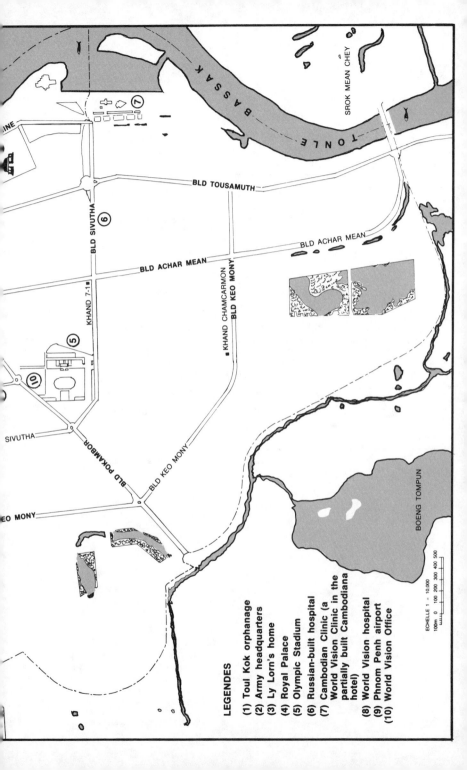

SROK MEAN CHEY

TONLE BASSAK

BLD TOUSAMUTH

BLD SIVUTHA

BLD ACHAR MEAN

BLD ACHAR MEAN

KHAND 7-1

KHAND CHAMCARMON

BLD KEO MONY

SIVUTHA

BLD POKAMBOR

BLD KEO MONY

KEO MONY

BOENG TOMPUN

ECHELLE 1 = 10.000

100m 0   100 200 300 400 500

LEGENDES

(1) Toul Kok orphanage
(2) Army headquarters
(3) Ly Lorn's home
(4) Royal Palace
(5) Olympic Stadium
(6) Russian-built hospital
(7) Cambodian Clinic (a World Vision Clinic in the partially built Cambodiana hotel)
(8) World Vision hospital
(9) Phnom Penh airport
(10) World Vision Office

3

Hope in the North

For the Cambodian people, families are the reason for living. My aunt's children were like my own brothers and sisters, and now we were afraid because we were not sure where they were. If we did not have them, it was possible that we had no living relatives — and that was unthinkable, so we hid among the trees while everyone else was put on the train.

Very early the next morning we were awake, putting together the few things we still possessed in order to prepare our family for the journey to Battambang Province. We were excited, and the children looked forward to the change. We felt we had a new chance, an opportunity to begin again, and the glimmer of hope in Father's eyes made me happier than anything else could have. It was about ten kilometers to the rendez-vous point, and we were there ahead of schedule.

It was a surprise to see hundreds of others there and realize that many villages were involved in the move. There were at least thirty trucks, but no drivers. As we waited, people wandered around, sometimes seeing a familiar face, and aching for a conversation. The soldiers would not tolerate much of this, but we could discuss where we had been living and how we were feeling. We had to be careful, though, not to say anything against the revolution.

Everyone was wondering what had been happening in other parts of the country. We knew we would be riding through Phnom Penh en route to Battambang Province and were anxious to see if the city had changed. I sensed a new hope around me. We all knew that something better was ahead of us because the main leader, after all, was waiting to welcome us. I secretly wondered if he had houses ready and what our new life would be like. Mother had talked me into giving up to a distant cousin of hers some of the clothes I had taken to

Takeo, but I still had my favorite clothes, make-up, high heeled shoes, and New Testament. I felt ready for a new life in Battambang.

We waited for two days for the drivers to arrive. Those nights were very dark, and we slept with only the trees for shelter. We took turns holding Nan's baby, trying to keep him warm with our bodies. When it rained, we gathered under a tree to stay as warm and dry as we could. Since Mother had brought some rice and a pan with her, we were able to prepare a small amount each night before the sun went down and darkness set in.

Finally the drivers arrived and we began to gather around trucks, ready to get this phase of our journey started. Some of the drivers seemed nice, but most of them showed contempt for us—just as the soldiers had done. I was surprised when the soldiers said, "Put your baskets and belongings on the ground. All this baggage will be brought to you in a separate truck." We didn't trust these men, so began picking out the warmest pieces of clothing and putting on as many layers as possible. I had to leave my favorite shoes in the bag, but was able to keep my New Testament and some lipstick in my clothing. Mother managed to keep the rice, a little bit of other kinds of food, and the cooking pan with her.

The Khmer Rouge were very rude—going through the crowd, using their guns to push us onto the trucks. They did not count how many people went on each one, but just kept shoving until there was no more room. Before my father realized what had happened, we were on one truck and my aunt, her family, and my dear Grandmother were on another. Father motioned to a soldier going by and said, "Please, let those people on our truck. They are our family." He rather nicely responded, "Don't worry. All the trucks are headed for the same destination." We believed him.

This was not the way I had envisioned the beginning of our new life in Battambang. I whispered to Nan, "This is like a nightmare and just as bad as anything they've done to us." She only nodded in agreement as she tried to comfort her hungry baby.

At least one hundred of us were stuffed into each truck. No one could sit down. As we stood, bodies pressed together, we realized that it would be worse when the rains came—there were no roofs on the trucks.

Driving away from the meeting site, I felt sorry for the people who had been forced to leave valuables and I was thankful that we had our little bit of gold hidden in our clothing. The soldiers did not even wait until we were out of sight before they gleefully began rummaging through the bundles, taking whatever they wanted. As I suspected, none of us would ever see those things again. I wondered if we would always be helpless to fight against these torturers.

The truck drivers were young boys who must have had to learn to drive very quickly. Many holes and bumps made the road rough, and because they drove so fast and recklessly, the ride was very uncomfortable. As we bounced along, I became more uneasy and wondered where this was leading us.

Why would the main leader, who had asked us to come to him, allow us to be treated this way? Silently, I prayed again for strength and protection for us all.

The stench in our truck became great because our driver would not stop for people to relieve themselves, which had to be done standing up in the middle of that crowd of one hundred. Babies were crying from the hunger we all felt; people were frustrated and angry. Our legs hurt from standing so long and we were desperate for some relief from the situation, but we knew there was nothing we could do about it.

When the truck behind us went over a bump very fast, a woman suddenly screamed, "My baby! My baby!" Her baby had bounced out of her arms and into the road. Merciless, the driver refused to stop so that she could pick up her child. She never knew if her baby died right away or not. The driver's orders were to drive, and that was all he would do. I was glad that Nan was not that mother.

As we approached Phnom Penh, we were all filled with anticipation and curiosity, wondering how it might have changed in the last four months. I remembered our home and the last time I had walked through its familiar rooms. I wondered how it looked now and whether anyone was living there. It was very strange to be riding through the city, especially on the back of a truck that reminded one of a cattle truck filled with people being treated worse than cattle.

I was shocked when I saw the deserted streets. There were no cars or bicycles, no people laughing and talking, no horns honking or dogs barking. The front doors of stores and homes were open, and it looked as though someone might come out at any moment. Buildings were damaged. The grounds had not been kept properly, the grass was high, and in some unlikely places, banana trees had been planted—to conserve space, I suppose. The streets were heavily littered with debris, garbage, and various items of furniture and decorative pieces that had been taken from homes and buildings. The piercing silence was most penetrating. Altogether it reminded me of ghost towns I had seen in movies. We felt the silence, but could only see a few Khmer Rouge soldiers in their drab black uniforms.

Someone on the truck said they had heard that anything of value or that showed the Western influence had been taken from homes and burned. We were shocked when we saw good, sometimes new, cars in the river, and throughout the city other cars that were obviously deserted. As we rode out of the city, we saw a "car cemetery." There were hundreds of cars, some of them new and all piled together, reduced by now to rusted-out rubble. The one thing that all these cars had in common was their missing tires. Civilization had no place in Pol Pot's regime, but the tire was useful for sandals because they would last forever.

The rains I had feared when we left Takeo Province did come—in torrents. We all huddled around Nan and her baby to keep them as dry as possible. Pushed close together, wet, and hungry, we were more tired than I would have believed, and since the muddy roads made the truck slip around even more, the whole ride was filled with misery. After several hours the legs of some of the old people simply gave out, and when they collapsed on the floor of the truck, people around them had no choice but to step on them. Some died this way, but the drivers would not stop to remove the bodies. They just kept on driving—the faster the better.

After thirteen hours of riding without one stop, we finally arrived at 3:00 A.M. in Pursat Province. Our first thought was to find a way to make a fire and fix some of the rice that Mother had brought with her. Others had done the same, thus many people were devouring their food when the soldiers began walking among the groups of people shouting that it was time to board the train for our final destination.

Again they said that the main leader was there and waiting to welcome us. I wanted that to be true so much that I believed them and convinced myself that kind people were anxious to help us make this place in Battambang Province our new home. As more people arrived at the makeshift train station, we realized that many others were also going toward Battambang. (Later we learned that more than 30,000 had been sent to that area.) There we hoped we would be able to live peacefully and grow the rice to fill the stomachs of our families, now the priority of us all.

When the train arrived, my family did not go on board because we were waiting for the truck on which Grandmother and my aunt's family were riding. I worried about Grandmother, wondering if the rains had been too much for her and had made her sick. I looked at Father and knew he was thinking the same thing. I went to him and he put his hand on my shoulders. "It's going to be all right," he said softly. I think he was trying to reassure himself as much as me.

As Father went to stand by Mother, I overheard him say, "She needs me to be near her. I never should have allowed them to put her on a different truck. Once we are together again, I will be sure that Grandmother always stays with us." He knew that he was her favorite and that Grandmother always felt safe with him. He had always been able to give us all that feeling of security.

For the Cambodian people, families are the reason for living. My aunt's children were like my own brothers and sisters, and now we were afraid because we were not sure where they were. If we did not have them, it was possible that we had no living relatives—and that was unthinkable, so we hid among the trees while everyone else was put on the train.

We waited all that day and watched as different groups of people came and went. Father decided we would wait one more night for the trucks in which our family was riding, desperately hoping that they had not gone on a different road. Early the next morning we heard the soldiers say that the rest of the trucks from Takeo were coming.

"They'll soon be here," Mother whispered. A tingle of excitement went through us all. As the trucks approached, my eyes were anxiously looking for Grandmother and assurance that she was well. There were about twenty trucks in the convoy, and I spotted my aunt in one of the first. I was excited until I realized they were not stopping. The trucks slowed down because of some people in the road. I saw an unforgettably helpless look on Grandmother's face when she saw us but realized the truck was not going to stop.

It would have been very dangerous for us to say anything, so all we could do on that day in July 1975 when we last saw those dear members of our family was wave an "I love you." With tears streaming down our faces, my parents, brothers, sisters, and I clung to each other. We were together but felt such a deep sense of loss and loneliness because so much of our hope and strength had just been taken away in that truck and we didn't know where it was going.

Father said, "The soldiers knew that we loved those members of our family. They separated us for a purpose, but we still have each other. We'll work and fight together." The frustration of our inability to change the unchangeable again settled heavily upon us.

With no further reason for hiding out at the Pursat train station, we mingled with the next group to board the train heading toward Battambang. That ride was another frightening experience—the kind I never got used to. Again we were crowded together and treated with total contempt by the soldiers. Their actions made me admit to myself, *I have been dreaming. There is no one waiting in Battambang to welcome us. I don't know where God is in all of this. I don't know why He is allowing these people to treat us this way.* A cold, icy fear settled on us all, and we tried to prepare ourselves and each other for what the soldiers might do to us that we had not already experienced.

Approximately 180 kilometers north of Phnom Penh the train stopped at Ocret—a very tiny town between Pursat and Maung. In the eyes of almost everyone around us there was defeated resignation, and at that moment I felt that we were beaten.

Others felt that way, too, I think, but decided not to try to fight it or even to live with it. I heard stories of people who could not bear to go any farther than that train ride had taken them and, after getting off, threw themselves under the moving train and committed suicide. Some used other methods, and many wished for the chance.

As we walked along the National Highway, I had no idea that it would be four years before I would see it or anything comparable, because until we were told to begin walking toward it, I had not realized we were going to live in the forest. *The forest.* How could we do

Lorn and a baby under her care at WVI (1974)

that? We were city people. I recalled stories of the wild animals and all sorts of creatures that lived in the forest, but people? My family? I still could not reason out how these fellow Cambodians who called themselves Khmer Rouge could do this to us. I tried to understand why they were being so cruel, what they had to gain by forcing us out of our homes and towns and into the forest, but there was just no answer.

It was August 1975. I was twenty-one years old as we walked through the heavy rain toward our new "home"—was it possible it would be the secure, happy place I had dreamed of for so long?

The Khmer Rouge wanted us to be totally remote from any sign of civilization, so we walked for two full days—about fifteen kilometers—into the forest. The deep mud made it necessary for us to carry the children. Mother and I took turns carrying Tak. As I held him close, giving both of us a little comfort, I remembered the day he had been born in Phnom Penh. That was a happy day and reminded me of other experiences from that time in our life. Looking around at the several hundred people walking with us, I saw many I could have met in the Phnom Penh marketplace a few months before. In this foreign world of the forest, it almost seemed that the experiences brought back by these memories had happened to someone else, and it was difficult to remember any details of our life in the city.

Even though Phnom Penh and my friends seemed a million years—rather than four months—away, in my heart I knew that those memories were mine and that not even the Khmer Rouge could take them from me. They would give me strength.

A view of the World Vision Hospital in 1974

Photo by E. Mooneyham

4

Phnom Penh As I Loved It (1970–75)

This was a sad experience, but it helped me realize that God had brought people from different parts of the world to demonstrate His love to the people of Cambodia in our time of need. He was giving us the chance to know Him by having these people become a part of our lives. I realized in a new way how much I could trust Him. No matter what happened, I would never be alone.

My first recollections of Phnom Penh are not happy because in 1970 we had been forced to move from our lifelong home, Ang Tasaom, to the city. I was sixteen, and going from the sedateness of country life to the sophistication of big-city life in Phnom Penh filled me with great fear.

I remember riding into town one day. Needing something solid to hold onto, I clutched the sides of the motorbike and looked to Father for extra support. He could always give it to me with a special smile and look in his eye that I thought was reserved just for me.

The number of refugees camped by the road overwhelmed me. Some were in large camps and others in small family groups. I had not been prepared for such a scene and felt sorry for them but thankful I was not facing their situation. As the days passed and I saw refugee people in different parts of the city, I thought about how it must feel to be so destitute, and I wished there were a way I could help them.

As soon as we arrived in Phnom Penh, we went to the home of my mother's sister. There was a happy reunion, and we were soon settled in and made to feel at home. Father and I then went off to his cousin's shop downtown. The department stores of Kim Hok Sé had the reputation throughout Phnom Penh of having anything one could need or want from cosmetics to televisions. I was instantly enamored and began having dreams of someday following in my aunt's footsteps.

Within a few days we had found a small house to rent on a nice quiet street. It had three bedrooms, a kitchen, and a living room. Best of all, it was right next door to the home of one of my aunts, and Grandmother was going to live with her.

Hy, Phanny, and Heng were involved with school activities, and Houng and Peo stayed home with Mother. We were all glad for the chance to begin again after the heartbreak of having to leave our home in the countryside.

It was a good life in Phnom Penh. The fabric store Father's cousin had helped us buy opened at 7:00 every morning, and I thrived on the challenge of the business world. The days went by very quickly and I was always surprised when Father announced, "It's 6:00 P.M. Time to close the shop, Lorn."

Nan is an excellent seamstress and her designs added a new dimension to the business Father and I had first developed in Ang Tasaom and carried on in Phnom Penh. Soon we had an excellent reputation throughout the city. All of this happiness—coupled with the fact that Tak was born within six months of our arrival in Phnom Penh—made me believe that we could have a very happy future as city people. I dared to hope that the war would stay away from the security of our little world.

As the months went by, we learned to enjoy the freedom and comforts that came with living in the city. We children continued to be very close friends with our cousins and even made new friends with the neighbors. The business grew, and Mother filled her life by loving us all.

Still, we all knew the meaning of the thunderous sounds of war that were almost always in the background. This caused us to worry about the people in the countryside—those whose lives were endangered by the bombs and rockets we had narrowly escaped. We all wondered where and when it would end so that we could go back to Ang Tasaom and the life we really wanted to live.

By 1972 the financial pressures in Phnom Penh had become great. Everything we needed rose in price, and we all had to work harder and longer hours than ever. Tensions were high every place we went. As a family we became lonesome for the peaceful life of the country but had to accept the fact that it would be longer than we had anticipated before we could return to Ang Tasaom. City life was good to us, but so much different than we were accustomed to, more crowded and complicated, more rushed and impersonal. We seldom shared relaxed, carefree evenings with my aunts and uncles because people just didn't take time to do that in the city.

One compensation of the higher economy was that our business did very well. As it expanded and we took on more varieties of fabrics, we continued the long, hard hours in order to make and sell as many pieces of clothing as possible. Sometimes I wished we could relax and enjoy the profits, but Father was very wise and realized that we needed to make and save as much as we could—while we could.

It was in these days of turmoil that Nan first met Meng, an electrician who lived and worked near our home. After asking a mutual Chinese friend to arrange a meeting with my parents and Nan, Meng began coming to our home. Following the strict Cambodian custom, Nan would not allow Meng to see her without one of our parents present. As we became more acquainted with him, we learned that Meng's village had also been taken over by the Khmer Rouge. He had escaped, but his parents had not. They had been forced to stay there and become a part of the rebel forces. After his third visit to our home, Meng wanted to ask for permission to marry Nan. Because he did not have a family to accompany him on this mission—another Cambodian custom—he asked several of the old people in our town to join with him. We knew the purpose of their visit, so my parents asked Nan if she wanted to marry Meng. This is a decision for which we traditionally trust our parents and Nan wanted to leave it to them. She said, "If you think it's a good idea, I want to marry Meng."

Friendship with a man was all new and frightening for Nan, so the two months that Meng was "calling on her" were not especially happy. She and Mother spent a lot of time together during those days and Nan was able to share both her fears and hopes with Mother. Even though Nan and Meng did not yet have a strong love for each other, as a family we liked Meng and knew that it was right for them to be married. The love would follow when they really knew each other.

Of course, they did not have much money, so Mother and Father decided the newlyweds should live with our family for the first year to help them get a good start financially before they began their own family. Our house was a little more crowded that year, but we had good times together and were all glad for the chance to become acquainted with Meng.

In 1973 Nan and Meng decided it was time to be on their own, so they moved to Kompong Som. We were all happy for them and looked forward to Nan's cheery letters to the family. She missed being with my parents and the family and often sent gifts to remind us of her love.

Nan worked at the market in Kompong Som, buying a few things with her own money and then selling them later when she could get a profit. She did quite well at this and always seemed happy.

About the same time Nan left Phnom Penh, I began to study English, with the encouragement of a few friends who had already begun the course. Even though I had to pay for classes in a private school, I was determined to spend the five hours a week—and some of our hard-earned riels—to prove to myself that I could learn English.

My life began to revolve around working, studying, and sleeping. It seemed that I was always doing one of those three things, but the sense of achievement with my English thrilled me.

After just a few months of study, I heard about a lady named Ruth Patterson who taught a Bible class (in English!) at a place called Bethany Church. I told my friend, "I've heard of the Bible and would like to understand it better. I think I will go to the classes." I think she knew, though, that even more than understanding the Bible, I wanted the free English lessons.

I faithfully spent one-and-a-half hours, five evenings a week, listening to the story of Jesus Christ and His love—in English. I could hardly absorb all I learned, but for more than five months I told myself I was there only to study English under a British teacher. It took that long for me to realize I wanted to personally know the meaning of God's love. Miss Patterson told me that "He can make you feel peaceful and joyful in your heart.

He wants to take away your worries and fears, and He only asks that you accept Him and His love." I did accept Jesus Christ and began to learn the meaning of His promises.

After English class one day, Miss Patterson told me about World Vision and their need for someone to translate for the English-speaking doctors and nurses— the perfect opportunity to practice my English. More important, I would finally be able to help the refugee population that had grown considerably since that day we first came to Phnom Penh.

I accepted the position almost before it was offered to me and began by distributing medicines to patients, helping the doctors and nurses, and encouraging the patients. The main refugee camp, Cambodiana, was located about five kilometers from Phnom Penh. There were other smaller ones, though, and eventually I worked in the clinics in each camp. When other Cambodians wouldn't even touch them, the Westerners employed by World Vision and other relief agencies helped the refugees; and the refugees appreciated their love and dedication. Without the medical techniques, medicines, vitamins, and help in getting food, many more refugees would have died.

Dr. Pene Key, a friend of Miss Patterson, was responsible for setting up the entire program for World Vision. During the two years that I worked with them, the team of medical people grew from 60 to 125 loving, professional people. Many of these were Cambodian and there were about twelve doctors and nurses from Western countries. I was very proud and happy to be a part of this wonderful group.

The most difficult job each day was to decide when

we were finished and who would be our last patient. The lack of food and the basic necessities of life made major health problems out of what should have been minor irritations, so our clinics were always full and overflowing. No matter where we stopped, there was always a long line still waiting, and I had a gripping fear that some of the people we had not been able to help would not have the strength—or even be alive—to come back the next day. I often wished I could keep saying "just one more," but that was impossible.

To some we were the last resort. I remember one refugee whose husband had been killed, leaving her with three little children. By the time she heard about our clinic, only one child was still alive. Orsovanna was three years old and had *kwashiorkor* (the result of a severe protein deficiency that causes the body to swell because the tissues are filled with fluid). The doctors gave him injections that strengthened him. Good milk and vitamins every day for several weeks helped, too. We were even able to put him in our children's nutrition center, Tuol Kok, for a few days. It was a joy to watch as his body became strong, his color good, and his face happy.

Every time I saw Orsovanna, he remembered me and called me "teacher." That was a sign of respect. I came to love that little boy in a special way, worrying when we did not see him or his mother for several days. Finally they came to us one day. She was carrying two small gifts, one for the doctor and one for me. We knew her pride would be hurt if we didn't accept them, so we took the little treasures from Orsovanna's mother and slipped some extra milk and vitamins into the little bag she was carrying.

Every day of working with these people was filled with rewards, and I was pleased when Hy joined our team to share them. He was big and strong, but his job at the clinic was to weigh and measure the tiny malnourished babies for the doctors. Proud to tell everyone that he was my brother, I can still see him—handling each little one with such gentle, loving care.

Sometimes after work I would go to visit the children at Tuol Kok Nutrition Center. I loved holding them, playing with the strong ones, and helping nurse those who were very sick. Sometimes these were abandoned children whose desperate parents, obviously without hope of being able to keep them alive, had left them at the home and run away. Often the little ones were so weak they could not even make the sound of a cry, but the look in their hollow eyes was all I needed to know that their little bodies were racked with pain. They came to us with every sort of problem—dysentery, typhus, tuberculosis, malaria, various infections, and, of course, kwashiorkor.

Many of these babies reached us after their symptoms had advanced and then we could be of little help. Each time one died it was a very emotional experience for all who had worked to save that life. I often assisted an Australian nurse, Isabel Broad, and remember one specific baby whom she had nursed round-the-clock for days. The baby had symptoms of several major diseases, but the basic problem was that he had been starving for so long that he was susceptible to everything. Early one morning that baby died. We all wept, for we had so much wanted that little child to live. Isabel felt as though he were her own, and she used her personal money to pay for the baby's funeral, which we all attended with her.

This was a sad experience, but it helped me realize that God had brought people from different parts of the world to demonstrate His love to the people of Cambodia in our time of need. He was giving us the chance to know Him by having these people become a part of our lives. I realized in a new way how much I could trust Him. No matter what happened, I would never be alone.

In 1974 rumors spread that soldiers were kidnapping and raping girls who walked alone at night. This was the first time I had reason to walk with fear. Even though we sometimes worked very late at night, the doctors with whom I worked were careful that I never went home alone. When my mother heard the rumor, she declared, "I will never go to bed until you are safely at home." Even though I was grown, she loved me so much and wanted to protect me from harm. There was a strong love between us, and even though she is no longer alive, the bond between us is still very real.

Father sold the fabric store in early 1974 and began a business similar to Nan's. He was good at this, and, because he was not very strong physically, it helped for him to be able to set his own pace and work hours. The intense pressures had caused Father to develop an ulcer, so we all encouraged him to rest and let us do the work. A proud man, he would not let us take his responsibility, but at least this work was somewhat easier for him.

In October 1974 the family received good news. Nan was pregnant and we were all going to be aunts and uncles and grandparents! I don't know who among us was the most proud, but we all anticipated the happy day and looked forward to her every letter. Sometimes she would tell us she was feeling sick in the mornings. One letter said, "Today I felt the baby move for the first time. Meng and I are very excited to have our own child."

Sometimes we worried. Meng was spending most of the daylight hours in hiding for fear of being forced to become a part of the forces, because any young, strong man on the streets of the towns outside Phnom Penh was seen as a candidate for military action. Nan and Meng had come to the conclusion that he must leave his job and stay at home. Nan's work at the market gave them the money they needed, but as the months went by, life became more difficult and they lived in constant fear of what could happen to Meng.

In March of 1975, Mother wrote Nan and told her she should fly to Phnom Penh. "The hospitals are the best here and the doctors are the most experienced. You must have these advantages with your first baby." Nan and Meng talked this over and decided she should come to us the second week of March. Meng stayed at home to take care of the house and save the expense of the high airfare. Also, it would have been dangerous for him to be seen on the streets or in the airport.

We were thrilled to see Nan. Mother loved "mothering" her and we all went out of our way to make her comfortable and happy. We knew that she missed Meng and felt bad to have left him in Kompong Som. A week or so after she arrived in Phnom Penh, Nan received a letter from Meng, who was lonesome and felt bad that it was impossible to come to her. The following week, the transportation and telephone services to Kompong Som were cut off, and Nan worried about how long that would last and when she would be able to return to Meng.

It was on April 5 that their son was born. We all loved this cuddly little baby immediately. Nan longed to be able to share the good news with her husband. "Communications and the transportation systems will be in operation again after the Cambodian New Year is over on April 16," Father assured her.

The Cambodian New Year, traditionally, was the happiest time of the year. We had three days off work, gave gifts, visited friends, celebrated with the traditional dances, and generally enjoyed family times. In 1975 it was different. We were under curfew. There was an eerie silence in Phnom Penh on both April 15 and 16. It was broken only by the whine of the rockets and loud popping of gunfire. April 17 was the day we were all forced to evacuate Phnom Penh and go to the birthplace of one of our elders.

Four months later, having been to Takeo and worked as laborers, we were headed into the forest and a life that I could not anticipate and for which I could not prepare myself or my family. I realized again that I was the only one who had the resource of God's strength, and I thanked Him that He was walking through that muddy forest with me.

I prayed for Hy, wishing that his commitment to Jesus was more complete. I watched Nan as she carried the baby, and thought of Meng, wondering if he was alive. I felt sorry that we had never been able to tell him about his baby. I felt sorry for Nan, knowing that she missed him so much and worried about his safety.

As I prayed for Meng, I prayed for my loved ones who

were scattered all over the country. *Dear God, the experiences of the last four months have taught me that the days ahead will probably require far more strength and determination to live than I've ever needed before. Please help me and help my loved ones wherever they are.*

គ្រូសារ

5

Learning To Be a Peasant

*My dream of security had faded so much
that I did not even remember it. Now
everyone I knew had only the goal of
survival. Even though it meant we had to
live like animals,
we fought to survive.*

*Not even the poorest refugee I had ever
seen in Phnom Penh had ever experienced
anything similar to the hell that was our
life in the forest. There was no end to the
inhumane persecution we experienced. We
wanted to be humans again, but we had to
live like pigs, with never a reason to be
happy. Eventually I realized that we were
no longer individuals with different
personalities. You couldn't tell one person
from another — some only survived longer
than others.*

The farther we walked into the forest, the more dense and frightening it became. It was a hot, humid August day. As I had feared, the "main leader" was not there. No one had welcomed us and there certainly were no houses waiting for us. Approaching the area where we would live, Hy said, "I feel like a pig going to slaughter." We were really afraid.

We could see that others had already arrived. Later we learned there were about thirty thousand people in this part of Cambodia with us. A few houses, standing on stilts and built close together, were in one section. We had heard that about four hundred people would live in our village and that it would be divided into about twenty units with ten families to a unit. The unit leader would be responsible for distributing the food, seeing to it that we followed orders, and deciding to whom anyone could report us if we said or did something that could be taken as against the Revolution.

Our only "welcome" was an order to begin clearing the small piece of land on which our house was to be built. The trees were very close together, and because we were given only an old, rusty hatchet, it was difficult to chop them down. My father and Hy did that part of the work while Phanny and the younger boys helped me gather the wood and bamboo to build the house. The large trees cut out of the forest to make the clearing would also be used for our house.

The process of building took two weeks. Even though

the rain fell almost constantly, we had no shelter and had to constantly eat, sleep, and live outside during those long days and nights. We slept on mats we made from the leaves of the palm trees. When they became filled with holes, we would simply gather new leaves.

Father, Hy, and I did most of the work on the house. When it was finished, it was about the size of one average bedroom. Father divided it with bamboo so that he and Mother could sleep in the back portion. It was so small, however, that they never really had any privacy.

When it was time to sleep, we simply put a blanket or piece of material on the floor over the leaves and lay down on it. Father had worked hard to thatch the roof well, so at least in those first few months we stayed dry even in the rainy weather. The most frightening part of life in the forest was the sound of unfamiliar animals in the night. I spent many hours awake, wondering when and how they attacked humans.

Heng, Houng, and Peo were forced to live away from home in a Communist-run school. Though not often, they were allowed some visits to us. When we were all together, some of us would sleep outside in hammocks made from pieces of material. It really didn't matter where we slept because this wasn't a real home to us and from the start we had felt that we were only existing, not living. My dream of security had turned into a plea for survival.

Since the house next to us was just a few feet away, it was impossible not to hear the people in it when they talked; we all understood the danger of saying anything that could be interpreted as disloyalty to the Revolution. The Khmer Rouge used many people—including children under twelve years old—as policemen. Actually, the society was designed to elevate the person who was able to accuse another of something they considered criminal, such as complaining about the lack of food, bad conditions, hard labor, or voicing memories of happy times.

Two times each week we had a meeting called the *ko sang* during which those who had been accused were forced to appear before the village people. After hearing the accusation, they were given the chance to admit their guilt. Sometimes the first appearance before the "ko sang" would not mean death, but there was no question about the second time.

Having an accusation to make brought great favor from the Khmer Rouge, so people became suspicious of their friends, and soon of their own family members. The Khmer Rouge wanted us to throw away our love and devotion to everything and everyone but Communism and the main leader.

An accused person sentenced to death was taken directly from the "ko sang" and never seen again. We would hear cries from the direction of the river. One of our neighbors told Father that ". . . these disloyal and uncooperative people are hit in the back of the head with a piece of bamboo until they die. Then they are pushed into the river." The ones who did not die immediately must have suffered great pain.

A woman with whom my mother had grown up and who was one of our "neighbors" was accused of complaining about the lack of food, when one of her children became especially ill. She was called in front of the "ko sang" one night, accused, taken to the river, and never returned to her children. Because her husband had already died, her small children were left completely alone. The soldiers did not care about them. Mother cried, "If only I could help them. . . ." If she had, certainly she would have been killed too. Those children never received answers to their questions about what had happened to their mother—they were just sent off to the regime's school, and we never saw them again.

This experience left an unforgettable impression on us as a family. Father said, "We must protect ourselves with a wall of silence. Be very careful even when you think we are alone as a family." We had to adopt the "see nothing, hear nothing, know nothing, understand nothing" philosophy. I now would add "feel nothing" to that list, since even that privilege was taken from us.

I had to learn not to speak—or even *think*—one word of English, Chinese, or educated Khmer—and had to live that way for the four years we were in the forest. We had to consciously erase from our minds everything that an even-barely educated or business-minded person would know. This was especially difficult for the children to understand. Father used very strong language to make them understand that even one wrong word could be very dangerous for them and for us all. "Until it becomes automatic," Father said, "we must work to blot the past from our minds. These soldiers are peasants and they love only peasants. If we want to continue living, we must become peasants."

This must have been especially difficult for some. I secretly recognized people around us as having been very wealthy in Phnom Penh. There were high leaders, businessmen, and educated people. What used to be an asset was now an element of great danger in their lives. In the early stages of the Khmer Rouge regime, everyone had been told to register on one of three lists: military, civil servants or intellectuals, and ordinary people. The first two groups were almost always killed without question. We were only told that they were "taken away," but the stories came back to us that they were either killed or put into a prison where they were treated with great brutality and usually died as a result.

Of course, we were given the impression that the professionals among us would have the opportunity to help build and run the new government. Those who did not sense danger, registered in their professional capacity. As time went on, we heard rumors that the goal of the Khmer Rouge was to purge our country of any Western influence and begin all over again—turning the Khmer calendar back to "year zero" and building a "revolutionary, pure, and rural society."

Sometimes the Khmer Rouge deceived people to find those who were not truly sympathetic with the Communist ideals. One day a friend of my father's told him this story:

> A group of soldiers in a nearby village gave the people the news of a mass killing—of men, women, and children—in another village. As they talked, they were closely watching the faces of the people. Anyone whose expression showed unhappiness with the news of this killing was taken away and murdered.

This friend, who wanted to be sure we understood how closely we were being watched, took a great risk in telling the story to Father. People had begun to realize that their educational background and professional experience were not assets, so everyone worked hard to forget all they had ever learned. But the Khmer Rouge soldiers were brutal in their persistence, using every tactic they could think of to identify those of us who were not truly peasants.

I was very aware of the fact that if it was discovered that I was a Christian, I would certainly be killed—and probably my family, too. The Khmer Rouge claimed that all Christians belonged to the CIA, and there was no way to escape the punishment for that crime.

We were told that everything was to be done for the Angkor, the ancient Khmer empire of the tenth century, which produced the beautiful city of Angkor Wat. Those kings had been considered divine and so was the anonymous Angkor—the Khmer Rouge—who would "decide our pathway to true happiness." We learned that a man named Pol Pot was the "main leader" and the one who had decided to create the "revolutionary, pure, rural society." One of our neighbors told Father, "Pol Pot is using a fairly small peasant army to kill all people who are influenced by Western countries, because he considers them impure. He wants to begin this new society with about one million people who will be under his control and influence." As Father shared that news with us, he was very sad. "That means," he said, "that he plans to let at least six million of our people die."

As I heard this information, I began to realize that the soldiers really meant it when they said, "It is better to kill an innocent person than to leave an enemy alone." We were told over and over that the only thing of value we possessed was our physical strength and that *that* belonged to the revolution. "When your strength is gone," one soldier shouted to us as we worked in the fields, "you are useless and ready to die." These were people who were cruel enough to cut a living man's body to pieces in front of his family.

For many months it was hard for me to accept the fact that these were my own people. They were also my enemies. Part of the price of being from the city was to be known as the worst enemy of the Khmer Rouge. We had to pay for our crime, they said.

One day Nan overheard a soldier ask an old man if there was anything he needed. The man responded, "Oh, thank you. I need some extra food for my family. They are very ill." When the soldier heard this, he became very angry, saying that he and the other Khmer Rouge people had gone for many years without enough food. His last words were, "You are all weak and lazy. You have lived too long in the city and deserve great punishment." The next person who was asked if he needed anything responded quickly that he and his family were fine. Many times we heard soldiers shout, "Prisoners of war! You are pigs. We have suffered much. Now you are our prisoners and you must suffer."

My dream of security had faded so much that I did not even remember it. Now everyone I knew had only the goal of survival. Even though it meant we had to live like animals, we fought to survive.

Not even the poorest refugee I had ever seen in Phnom Penh had ever experienced anything similar to the hell that was our life in the forest. There was no end to the inhumane persecution we experienced. We wanted to be humans again, but we had to live like pigs, with never a reason to be happy. Eventually I realized that we were no longer individuals with different personalities. You couldn't tell one person from another—some only survived longer than others.

Our day began when we were awakened by a bell at 4:30 A.M. We had to be at our place of work by 5:00 A.M. Soon after we arrived in the forest, I was assigned to work in a field about five kilometers from our house. Because it was rainy most of the time, everything was covered with mud, including me. I usually fell at least twenty times just going to work. We were not allowed to talk to the people around us while working or even while walking to work.

Arriving a few minutes late was cause for severe punishment—perhaps a beating, having to work without a midday break, or worst of all—having the day's rice allocation taken away. The heavy-handed discipline was enforced around the clock. We couldn't escape it.

It was uncommon to go to bed without hunger pangs, so we never slept well. Because we were not fed until noon, I sometimes wondered if I would be able to stand up through the whole morning.

Our rice portion for each day was usually one small cup of rice. At first they gave this to us separately while we were at work. After a few months they began a new system of having a central kitchen in which we all ate. The young soldiers guarding the food were told, "Be sure that no one eats too much." When they first began this process of having us eat in the central kitchen, the soldiers went through each house, searching for rice or anything people might have hidden to eat. Some families had saved a little bit here and there, and anything found was confiscated.

For many, intense hunger combined with the sameness of every day being like the one before, took away the desire to live. Many committed suicide. Men abandoned their wives and children, hoping they could escape the Khmer Rouge. As I watched all of the pain and fear around me, I tried to convince myself that survival was still worth fighting for, but sometimes that was very difficult.

I was forced to work like a man. The type of work assigned a person was decided by age, not by size, strength, or sex, so my work was the same as that of any other persons in their early twenties, male or female.

Most people were put into the fields—either planting or reaping the crop—but there were also canals and dikes to be built, baskets to be woven, rice to be husked, and children to be cared for. The various members of my family did these jobs and others. Sometimes we worked in the fields until dark and then returned to the village to learn that we had to husk the rice far into the night. "There is no relief" was the silent cry from throughout the forest.

One man we knew was given the duty of gathering all the villagers' excrement. He did this work for a full year from 5:00 A.M. until 6:00 P.M. His only equipment was a narrow board—not a shovel. The soldiers watched him closely, hoping he would do or say something for which they could punish him.

We were given three changes of clothing. Some of us managed to keep a few of the things we had brought from Phnom Penh. The regime's rule about clothes was that they had to be black—just like the ugly uniforms I had hated from the beginning of this nightmare.

We could do anything we wanted to make the clothes black, usually soaking them in the mud for a long time. The material given us by the soldiers was so thin and cheap that it tore very easily. I had kept a needle and thread, so was able to sew our things many times, but having to wear those dirty clothes only deepened the depression that nearly overwhelmed me.

Having no communication with the outside world was also a major problem. Father's portable radio had been confiscated a long time ago. And having no pencils, paper, or books added to our apathy. The soldiers had also taken away our soap, combs, and toothbrushes and made it very difficult for us to get access to the water supply. All incentive to keep ourselves clean or even think about our appearance had been taken away.

Probably the most significant aspect of life taken from us was the freedom to communicate with each other. We knew the spies were all around us at all times, so were never able to let down our wall of silence. I could be right next to my mother, but afraid to tell her what I was thinking. We had to learn to communicate with our eyes. Sometimes I would talk to myself, trying to gain strength, but usually I did not even have the energy or desire to do that. It was a real effort to think, to talk, or to make any movement not absolutely necessary.

Being young and shy, and feeling the weight of responsibility for my family when I longed to be dependent on someone else, I went as often as I could to the solace of my New Testament. It encouraged me. I tried to share the promises with my family, but it was almost impossible in our few stolen moments of communication to convince them that God loved them. I knew that He needed me to silently show His love to them.

Sometimes I dreamed of having a conversation with one of my Christian friends in Phnom Penh. If only there were some way I could talk—*really* talk—with someone who would understand and tell me what to do. It was in the midst of such desperation that I learned about prayer. I became very sensitive to God speaking to me, encouraging me, and loving me through situations that I had never noticed.

Many times I questioned God, praying silently, *Dear Lord, I don't understand why You do not feed my people the way You fed the five thousand with just a few loaves and fishes. I wonder if You are allowing these things to happen as a punishment for my country's failure to recognize You. I'm sorry for that, but I don't know how long I can go on living like this. Please help me.*

Of all the problems and pain we had to face, lack of food was the most basic. Different villages operated in different ways, but no one had enough to eat—except the soldiers, of course. At one point, Hy's job was to build a fence around the central kitchen. He would often come home very angry because he had seen the soldiers eating rice with vegetables, meat, or fish and leaving on their plates whatever they did not want. As they threw their leftovers in the fly-infested garbage can, they laughed and shouted at Hy, "Don't you wish you could be a bug and eat that good food?"

In one field we raised watermelons. I *love* watermelon. The soldiers were the only ones who got to enjoy them, and I would almost cry when the rinds were thrown away. The soldiers let me retrieve those rinds from the garbage and enjoyed watching me eat them—flies and all! They *wanted* us to act like animals.

In the central kitchen we were sometimes given plain rice; at other times, a gruel made of rice, green bananas, and red or white maize with strips of banana stems added. This was the food that country people gave their pigs, and when we ate it, the soldiers would shout, "You are pigs! You are pigs!" I can still hear those words and see the leer on their faces. Many days we were told, "There is nothing for you to eat unless you want this bran or paddy." (Paddy was unhusked rice and very difficult to eat.) On days like this it was tempting to eat the snails or paddy crabs we found in the fields. We knew they caused boils but we ate them anyway. Death was close and we would rather have died with full stomachs and boils than with empty stomachs and no boils.

When I was husking rice, I often ate handfuls of it raw. This always made me sick, but again, it was something in my stomach. Drinking a lot of water was another way to alleviate the hunger pangs for a few moments, but on a totally empty stomach the water made me very ill.

Mother's frugality saved our lives many times. Whenever we were given a little bit more than she felt we needed—or when we were able to steal some food that was not absolutely necessary for that particular day— she would hoard it until a time when we were desperate. There were many of those times. Her "supply" did not last forever, but it brought us through some sad, painful days.

Whenever I could sneak a few moments away from the watchful eyes of the soldiers and their spies, I would go into the forest, trying to find something we could eat. Usually it was leaves and roots, or if I was very lucky, a wild forest fruit. None of these tasted good, but we learned which ones could be eaten, and these helped postpone the inevitable—death.

LEARNING TO BE A PEASANT

Obviously, the use of any method of getting food other than the allotted amount from the central kitchen was punishable by death. I remember times people were killed for that reason or even for mentioning the lack of food. I was never surprised to see the body of such a person at the edge of the field. Sometimes I even saw the bones of one whose body had never been taken away. The cruelties—both mental and physical—were designed to beat us down to nothing.

We would not have minded the suffering if it had been for the good of our country or even if we had experienced a famine—then there would have at least been a reason for the pain. But we knew that rice was being put into storehouses. We had worked so hard to harvest the crops and then watched the oxcarts full of food going away from us. Sometimes I became angry but could only silently shout, *It's not fair!* Usually, though, I did not even have that much strength.

There was a black market in the forest. An especially desperate person could take something he had miraculously been able to save and trade it for rice. Father had managed to save several pieces of gold. One by one, he and Mother decided to use them for rice, but the rice went so fast—and then we had nothing. Even though the Khmer Rouge soldiers had organized this black market system to get from us anything of value, anyone involved in it, if caught, received the death warrant.

Whenever one of us was too sick to work, it meant a cut in our rice allotment. The next decision was how to divide what we did receive. The problem never caused a major disagreement in my family, but I remember that many others fought among themselves when this happened. I especially recall one of our neighbors who argued with his daughter about which of them needed the most rice. I first heard him shout, "You are my daughter, but you show me no respect. When you refuse to share your rice with me, you are saying you do not love me." When she responded, I could tell her feelings were hurt as she said, "You are an old man and do not work in the fields. I must work very hard every day. Without the rice, I do not have enough strength. I must have it to work. I must have it to live." That was when he beat her.

There were times when people thought the valuable bit of rice we received was useless because there was so little of it. I saw people angrily throw it on the ground, spit on it and say, "This is worthless." This reaction caused others nearby who would gladly have eaten it, to become very angry. Of course, the small amount we received each day wasn't enough to ease the hunger of even a small child, but one can understand the anger of a father who cannot fill the stomach of his child—or his own.

I thank God that I don't have memories of being hurt or hurting any of my family members with words. But we all struggled many times with what we should do. I remember praying silently, *Dear Lord, should I share my rice, knowing that I too may become weakened and unable to work? Father tells me not to share it, but to eat it and stay strong. It hurts so much to look at my parents and the little boys who are starving—and tell them that I cannot help. Give me the strength and wisdom I need, dear God.* He did give me strength, and I continued doing the best I could with what I had.

Within three months of our arrival in the forest, I was ordered to move away from my family and live in another village five kilometers from the family. This was another of their attempts to "break" us, and they almost succeeded. It was very difficult to be so far from my family. I spent many lonely hours, mainly worrying about what was happening to them—were they sleeping all right? Was anyone deathly sick?

Because we were not allowed to have real conversations, it was impossible for me to get acquainted with any of the people in this new village. Our mutual problems gave us an empathy for each other, and a few people were actually nice to me. Being alone, I could not have a house in this new place, so I hung a piece of material hammock-style. Rain or not, that was my bed—and my home.

By running both ways, I could cover the five kilometers during my midday break to see the family. Sometimes I would even sneak away at night to be with them. I managed to visit them at least twice a week. The added activity of having to travel that far made me more weak and more fatigued. I knew, though, that I needed the contact with them to maintain my sanity.

My job at the new village was to help build a canal. Pol Pot was actually trying to change the course of the rivers and canals in Cambodia because he didn't like the way they wound through the countryside. He wanted them to run straight like the grid marks on a map. Hy, Father, and I had done this work in Takeo and when we first went to the forest, so I knew what I was getting into when I received these orders. It was more back-breaking than I know how to tell. First I had to dig the dirt and put it into two large baskets. Next I had to put the baskets onto either end of a pole and hoist them on my shoulders and carry them to the assigned place.

Then I emptied the baskets and started over. It was such heavy labor that my hands and body became filled with blisters, sores, and bruises. (And I had thought it was hard to work in the fields!) When the monsoon season came, the dirt became mud and was heavier than ever. It was easy to slip and fall while carrying those huge baskets, and such a fall left no room for pride or modesty in a young, shy girl wearing a sarong.

When the torrential rains came, there was no place to get away from them, even to change clothes. Instead, we were forced to continue working. When the rains finally stopped, I would try to find a sunny spot to work so my clothes would dry, but they were so muddy that it was really hopeless. The exposure to this bad weather on a daily basis further weakened people, adding to the spread of malaria and cholera throughout the villages.

When the intense heat of January and February hit us, we had a different problem. It was so hot that one could easily faint from being in the sun without a hat, and the ground burned my feet even though I hadn't worn shoes for a long time. We needed the rice, so I kept on working.

The education of the village children began with the stories the women who took care of them were forced to tell. They were stories of how wonderful the Revolution was and the wisdom of the Khmer Rouge soldiers. Beginning at the age of six, the children were forced to attend the schools. The lessons taught them to love their country, the Revolution, and the Khmer Rouge. They were told to hate the Americans but love the workers and peasants who were their new parents. Houng, Heng, and Peo had to live at this school, but were usually allowed to see the family once a week.

They did not like the school. One day Houng told Mother, "We are told, 'You don't have to study, just work,' but Mommy, we want to study. We want to learn. But they make us work hard in the fields and they don't give us enough to eat." It broke my mother's heart to see her little boys suffer so much. But there was nothing any of us could do to help them. The Khmer Rouge had designed our work schedules to make it impossible to see them during the day. I didn't dare go to visit at a time when I would risk being late for work, because the punishment would have been a cut in rice allotment. If they had found that I had been to see the boys, it would surely have meant a prison sentence.

When I did sneak visits to the boys, I would always come back angry. The place where they had to stay was so dirty. There was nothing for the children to do but work. They were poorly fed, and no one was responsible to keep them clean or take care of them. Heng said, "We are told that our parents no longer have authority or responsibility for us. They tell us that Mommy and Daddy are to respect us and that our families are evil so we should be afraid to be near them. But we love you. We want to live with our family." I was helpless and told him he had to stay at school. They had to try to be strong. I wished I could do it for them.

One day in August 1976, I arrived at my parents' house to find that the boys had run away from the school. They just could not stand it any longer and needed the love and encouragement of the family. Because they were registered at the school and not with my parents, they were not allowed to receive any portion of rice while they lived at home.

That meant that Mother had to go to work in the

fields, even though she was not at all well. The work was very hard and she wasn't accustomed to using the sickle, especially when they forced her to work very fast. Actually, we all had cut ourselves with the sickle, but Nan and Mother were the most severely injured. The scar on my toe will always be a reminder of those long, hard days in the fields—and the fact that God kept that infection from taking my life.

Mother cut herself very badly. Without shoes or any protection for the wound, her foot became very sore. She would not complain, however, so we did not know how badly it was hurting. Father was too ill to work in the fields but was weaving baskets like the ones I used at the canal. I was especially sorry to be so far from Mother because after working in the fields, she had to go home and wash the clothes, carry the water, and do anything else necessary for the next day. I wished I could help her with those chores, but my visits with the family could be only a few minutes long.

The children had only been home a few days when Mother noticed Houng's arm was swollen. When she asked him about it, he said, "I did not want to worry you, but a snake bit me." His body was already weak from the slow starvation we were all experiencing. Once the infection was in his body, it spread rapidly. A friend of my father's gave him a root, whispering "Mix this with leaves and boil it to make a medicine. The swelling may go down." We were grateful for his kindness. The medicine worked, but only temporarily. We could only watch as Houng's body became more swollen.

I was amazed as I watched Mother's love grow with Houng's need. She made sure that someone was with him at all times. I remember hearing him beg through his tears, "Please, Mommy, let me be hungry until I die. It hurts to walk so far and work so hard. I get cold in the rain and I don't like to fall in the mud. I don't like to see you sad and I don't like to be hungry. Please, Mommy, just let me die." This made us all weep.

Mother did not know what to do for Houng. She knew she couldn't promise him that life would ever be better, and she wondered if she had a right to prolong his agony. None of us knew what to tell her.

Most of us could not even bear to look at the children. Seeing the hunger and pain in their eyes was worse than feeling the hunger and pain in our own stomachs. Instead, most people acted as if they didn't notice the hurting children. Father assumed this attitude as a way of defending himself emotionally, but Mother couldn't do that. She couldn't hide the heartbreak she felt when she saw us dizzy when we walked, because we had only air in our stomachs, or so hungry that our whole bodies ached, and we sometimes were so unhappy with life that we wanted to die. We all felt sorry for ourselves and for each other, but there was nothing to do except continue to survive as long as possible.

Precious Houng grew weaker and weaker. Every chance I could, I ran from the place where I lived to my parents' house. I tried to whisper to Houng about Jesus' love, and I still wonder if he ever understood what I was saying.

One day the leader in my village would not allow me to go visit Houng. I was angry but continued to work. The next day I went home and learned that he had died the day before. My heart was broken, and I openly complained to everyone around me that I was upset that

I had not been allowed to see my brother on the day he died.

Obviously, I was fortunate that those remarks did not cause one of the soldiers to have me killed, which would have been the normal course of action, because it was a crime to speak against the Communist leadership. My despair was so great, however, that I was not thinking logically. I only wanted to vent my feelings about the insanity of this life.

The situation was becoming more desperate. Mother was working but could barely walk because the infection had spread from her toe to her leg. Father was very weak and could not even weave the baskets any longer. Heng and Peo were both sick, and Nan's feet were so swollen from infected sores that she could not walk. Little Tak was almost six, but too small to be of much help. He followed Mother around like a little shadow when she was going to get food at the central kitchen, or doing the wash. When she was at work, Tak did what he could to help those who were sick. It was his sweet spirit that gave me the encouragement I needed at especially low points.

In the midst of our despair, I heard the bad news that Hy had been ordered to leave our family. He was to live and work in a village more than ten kilometers away. I had always depended so much on Hy. Even though he was younger than I, he was still my big, strong brother. When I learned that he had to leave the family, I asked God for the strength to take a big risk. I went to the leader of my village and begged, "Please give me permission to return to my parents' home. They need my help."

Phanny, who was also living away from the family,

made the same plea. We were both surprised but grateful to receive a "Yes. You may go." Of course, we each had to agree to accept less rice each day for the privilege of moving, but I silently praised God and asked for His help in taking care of these people I loved so dearly. Phanny and I were greatly encouraged to be together again. Even with the loss of Houng, the pain of our family, and the absence of Hy, the love we shared brought joy to us.

We worked hard in the fields from 5:00 A.M. until dark and used the rest of our time to try to make the sick ones comfortable—not an easy task. Not having any of the "conveniences" made it almost impossible to even get the fresh rags and hot water necessary to keep their draining wounds clean. I knew it was important to keep the insects from getting into the infected sores, but sometimes I was so tired and felt so weak that I didn't know where I would get the energy to help them another day.

Phanny was a blessing to us all. The Lord used her to lift me up from the very depths of the hell in which we lived. Nearly every time she came into the house, she managed to have some little thing to relieve us. Sometimes it was a piece of forest fruit. Other times she might have an extra bit of rice or a piece of fish that her "friend" the cook had given her. This woman wasn't a real friend, but she came about as close to Phanny as a Khmer Rouge came to anyone I knew. Everyone had always loved Phanny, though, so I shouldn't have been surprised that the cook recognized her as someone very special.

Even Phanny's remarkable spirit could not change the endless suffering we felt. As we watched our loved ones in pain, their bodies swollen and filled with open sores from the infections, we felt desperate and depressed. Malaria and typhus were all around us, and because of the unsanitary conditions and lack of shoes, these infections often spread from one person to another. There was no way to protect ourselves.

Sometimes I simply could not stand the pressures I felt closing in around me, and I had to be alone. There was no place to go, so I just sat in a corner, acting as though I couldn't see my family around me. I was angry and did not even want to communicate—by words or looks—with anyone. For many days my whole concentration would be on working to get food—nothing else, just working to get food.

After some weeks of living that way, I would come back to the reality of my responsibilities. Then I worried. Watching Father grow more and more lethargic, I thought I understood his feelings of emptiness, because deep inside, I knew that I needed to become the strong, responsible one to take Father's place.

Even when I wished for a way to share my feelings and fears, I knew it was impossible. We had to continue to remember the importance of the "wall of silence." The only time we could talk openly about anything except how much we enjoyed our work and the living conditions was when one of the family was sick. Then I could ask how they felt and what I could do to make them more comfortable for the next day. But there was nothing I could do to lift their morale—to really help them.

The weather added to our problems. It seemed as though it was always either very hot or very wet. I had trouble trying to remember how long we had been in the forest. Father kept track of the days for us and I would sometimes ask him what month we were in, usually because I wondered how much longer it would rain, or when the heat might let up.

Sometimes I was sure I was going crazy. I knew that I did irrational things, but had no control over them. Hunger can do that to a person. A few months of living in the forest had made me a very old woman. I was in my early twenties, but from looking at Nan and Phanny, I could tell that I must look more than fifty. I was tired, thin, sick, and frightened. We were treated like dirty animals, and I was beginning to feel and act like an animal.

When I was feeling comparatively strong, I could think really hard and remember our house in Phnom Penh. I thought about the furniture in our living room, the new television set, and my pretty bedroom. I wondered how I would look now if I could see myself in the long mirror, but I knew I didn't really want to know. I couldn't see my face, but I could tell that my body had changed, and I didn't like the way it looked.

It was September 1976 and it had been more than sixteen months since I had seen my parents laugh or talk happily. In some ways that hurt me the most. And I didn't think it would ever get better. I began to wonder if we should work so hard to survive, and what were we surviving for.

In my heart I knew that God was with me and that He loved me. John 3:16 came to me again and again. Sometimes I would wake up in the night, realizing that the verse had been going through my head even while I was sleeping. "For God so loved the world that he gave his only begotten Son, that whosoever believeth in him should not perish, but have everlasting life." No matter what the soldiers did to us, I had to remember God's great love.

I was thankful I had memorized so many verses, because when I was too weak to open my New Testament these passages came to my mind. When in the deepest agony, I remembered Miss Patterson's teaching, and I thought of David, who had suffered, too. So had Jesus. I knew He was with me and would carry me through these days. There was a reason for the experiences I was undergoing, and I had to keep fighting, one day at a time. I had to believe God would give me the strength and will to survive as long as He wanted me on earth.

6

No Hope for the Dying

Sometimes my prayer was, "God, I wish You would take us all right now, rather than taking us one at a time so that we have to watch our loved ones die. I really can't stand seeing them so sick. They're dying when there is nothing I can do to help. Please, take us all now, all at the same time."

The biggest shock facing me when I returned to live with my family was the deterioration of Father's health and spirits. While living away from home, I had noticed on my brief visits that he had become much weaker. It was not until I lived with my family again that I realized how critically ill Father really was. Because we had been such close friends, it hurt deeply that he would no longer talk with me or even communicate with his eyes. I did not know how to respond to this total silence and the way he had cut himself off from the rest of us.

Being unable to take care of us hurt him, because Father felt the family was his responsibility—not mine or anyone else's. It hurt more than his aggravated ulcer and the malaria from which he never recovered. He slept most of the time, or at least his eyes were almost always closed. I think that sometimes this was because he felt ashamed to look at us. He felt that he had let us down. Sometimes when I thought he was awake, I would try to say something to him, but Father would just stare straight ahead. I couldn't tell that he was looking at anything in particular. I hoped he was lost in dreams of happier days, because we were unable to do anything to help or cheer him.

In mid-September, just a few days after the death of Houng, a cut that Peo had gotten on his leg while at school began to look especially dangerous. It had not been kept clean at the school. When he arrived home, we cleaned it and worked very hard to keep it clear of mucous so that it did not attract the bugs. I thought it was going to be all right, but somehow it became infected. When we realized this, we made a medicine from a mixture of herbs, but the infection had spread too far and the medicine did not work.

As the infection raced through it, his body became more swollen. Soon our precious little eight-year-old was unrecognizable. When he could no longer walk, I often carried Peo out of the house so he could watch the people go by while I was at work.

When he lay there with the sun shining behind him, I could see through his skin. The swollen parts of his body were transparent and the water inside him was visible. There was constant, intense pain that heightened when he had to urinate or have a bowel movement, causing him to sob for some kind of relief.

Every part of his little body hurt, and as I helplessly watched, I felt my emotions pulled in every direction. I was angry at the Communists and at life. I could not understand why my innocent little brother, who had not even had a chance to live, was suffering so that these cruel Khmer Rouge could achieve their goals. This certainly did not seem to me like the way to build a "pure rural society." I was very angry. God would often remind me, *I love these little boys even more than you do.* I couldn't make it all come together in my mind but knew I had to accept the situation and leave my little loved ones in His hands.

Another day in mid-September Nan, Heng, Father, and Peo were all sick and trying to rest in the house. No one was talking, but when they heard Peo's strange, loud gasp for breath, Father told the others, "Our little Peo has died. He will suffer no more. He will never again be hungry." Nan and Heng could not believe he was really gone, but Father had recognized that sound of death. Heng crawled over to Peo. He tried desperately to wake him and finally admitted to himself that his brother had died.

Nan called out the door, "Please get my mother and sisters from the field. My little brother has just died." Surprisingly, we were given permission to go home. We were sad that we had not been with this little one in his last moments. Mother cried, "I wish I could hold him once more and see his sweet smile." We prepared Peo's tiny body for burial, wrapping it carefully and with great love. Mother, Phanny, and I carried him to the place where we were told to put his body. It was very difficult to leave his body in the shallow grave someone had dug for us.

Our consolation, Phanny reminded us, was that our little Peo would never again cry in pain, but it was hard to think of life without Peo's loving ways. He had always been the one who liked to cuddle. Even when he was sick and hungry, the human touch could bring a smile to his lips; and wherever I was sitting, he would come near me. I still miss him deeply and think of him often.

Mother sometimes talked about the possibility of her own death. I don't believe she feared it for herself, but she loved us so much that the thought of not being with us—especially if we were suffering—was too much to bear. When she spoke of death, it was as though she was trying to prepare us for the day when she would no longer be there to comfort, love, and help us.

Sometimes my prayer was, "God, I wish You would take us all right now, rather than taking us one at a time so that we have to watch our loved ones die. I really can't stand seeing them so sick. They're dying when there is nothing I can do to help. Please, take us all now, all at the same time."

I could not understand why God had created the Khmer Rouge and why they were better off than we were. I wished there were a way that I could get even with them, but it was hopeless—they were many and I was only one. These thoughts came to my mind many times, night and day. Soon after, they were followed by God's promise, "I will never leave thee nor forsake thee." It was to this that I clung.

Within a week after Houng's death, Heng began to have dreams whenever he fell asleep. He was so weak that he slept often and, I think, was delirious from lack of food combined with the uncomfortable living conditions. By this time we usually just slept on the wood, not having the strength to pick the leaves for a bed. Sleeping was not at all comfortable.

We had dug a hole under the house and put a small board on either side of it so we could use it to go to the bathroom, but when one of us could not get down the stairs to go under the house, we had to allow our bowels to move whenever necessary. Phanny and I would have to wash the floor and the hurting bodies when we got home.

The biggest problem was that there was no hope for the future. Heng realized that, so he allowed himself to sleep and to dream. In these dreams, Houng spoke to Heng and told him how much rice and other food he had in his new home, and how it was warm and comfortable. Houng chidingly said, "Heng, why do you want to live such a sad life when you could choose to come with me and be happy?" Night after night Heng had these dreams and day by day he became weaker.

When Peo became ill, Mother sold our two mosquito nets to the black market for five tins of rice. That decision made me very sad because Heng was so weak he could not even wave the flies away, and they were eating him up. Those five tins of rice had not been very helpful—now we suffered because we did not have the nets. I became angry with Mother. I wanted to shout, "Why did you give up those valuable nets for that little bit of rice?"—but of course I didn't say a word.

The mosquitoes were biting all of us. I was sick too. As I lay there looking at my loved ones—all of us pale and nearly dead—I could not understand which of us even had enough blood to make the mosquitoes stay in our house. Soon I found myself talking to them— pleading with them, "Please don't bite me. I have nothing for you." None of us had. But not even the mosquitoes would have pity on us. They kept biting, and malaria spread through our family again and again.

I knew that I had to get back to work because we needed the rice. Phanny had remained strong, but I couldn't let her do everything alone. Soon I was back at it. Because everyone else was sick, Phanny and I had to get up to 4:00 A.M. instead of 4:30 A.M. We wanted to get everything ready so that our family would be all right while we were away from them for the day. We would haul water to the house and get fresh rags; and when we could find food, we gave them something to eat. With these things at hand and Tak to help—Mother and Nan were able to take care of each other, Father, and Heng.

When we came home, we would clean their wounds and, if necessary, their hurting bodies. Whenever possible, we would help them down the stairs to go to the bathroom, then we would go to the central kitchen to get whatever food was to be given us that day and then divide it up among our family members. Phanny and I would then return to the field to work until dark before going home and preparing for the next day.

I was glad that at this time I was harvesting in a field not quite ten minutes from our house, so I could run quickly to the family every possible chance. The work was back-breaking, but sometimes I was able to steal a little of the corn, cabbage, or potatoes that we were harvesting and take it home to the family. Many times we ate the vegetables raw, without even washing them.

Shortly after Peo's death, Mother's toe infection became worse and she could no longer work. This, of course, took away some of our rice allotment. I was the one who had to divide what we were given, to try to keep us all alive. I was glad, though, that Mother was home all day so she could be there with Father. Even though they could not have real conversations, and Father still did not even want to talk to us, I was glad that at least my parents were together. We could see Father becoming more and more thin, and we all knew that he would soon die.

I went to the central kitchen and begged. The cook gave me a little extra rice for Father, but he was too sick to eat it. He did talk to me, though. I'll never forget his words as he said, "Daughter, I know that I am going to die very soon." I protested saying, "I will beg again, I will steal if necessary to get the food we need." He responded, "No, I do not want that. I have already been too much of a burden to you and the others, but I do beg you to remain strong and take care of your mother and the rest of the children. Please do not complain too loudly about the Khmer Rouge anymore. I am afraid they will surely kill you." He knew how close I had come to death after complaining about not being able to see Houng before he died, and he did not want me to take that risk again.

The morning that Mother woke me to say that Father was no longer with us was a very sad one. I didn't tell her but silently wondered how I could live without Father. Even though he had been very weak and uncommunicative these last months, he had been there. He had given me a reason to survive. Now Father's place in the house would be empty and so would a large place in my heart.

Father had been too weak to talk to Mother just before he died, so she was only able to lie next to him and hold his hands as she listened to his raspy breathing in that last hour. Because she did not have the strength, Mother asked me to change his clothes and put clean ones on him before we buried him. As I did this, she cried and cried, desperately feeling the loss already. She missed Grandmother and our other relatives, too. Over and over she said, "Think how sad they would be if they knew he had died. He was the favorite and now he lives no more."

As with Peo and Houng, we wrapped Father's fully-clothed body with cloth. He was too heavy for me to bury by myself, so I waited for the leader to ask some of the other refugees to come and help me. They carried his body out of our house and to the gravesite by tying his hands to one end of a long stick and his feet to the other end. I wished that Mother did not have to watch his body being taken away like that, and was sorry that neither she nor Nan could walk as far away as we would have to go to bury him.

Phanny and I tried to be brave as we walked behind these men and watched them dig the hole for our father's body. It was a quiet, cloudy day. I remember noticing that the trees were especially beautiful. Father would have loved the colors. If it had not been such a sad day, it would have been lovely, even in the forest. After the hole was dug, they put his body into it. I wished there were a way to have a casket, but that was impossible. When they began putting the dirt on top of him, something in my heart seemed to stand still. I realized then that he was really gone. I could never again see his face or hear his voice. This realization hurt more than I can describe. When we returned home and told Mother about the burial, I could see that something had gone out of her eyes. The loss of Father meant something to her that we could not understand. I only knew that she would never again be the same.

But we had to go on living. I felt the responsibilities more heavily than ever. Heng was very sick with an illness different from Peo's. Looking at him, Phanny said to me, "Heng is so thin that his bones stand out from his body. I can count his ribs, and his legs and arms are like sticks—just bones covered with skin. There is no fat or muscle at all. What can we do, Lorn, to help him?" I could only turn and walk away because I didn't have an answer.

Mother's sickness, combined with depression from losing Father, caused her to remove herself from us. She would not talk to me or give me any idea about what I could do for Heng. I felt lost. I did not have medicine or good food, and our house smelled bad all the time.

Every time we breathed we became a little more nauseated. I knew it was impossible for Heng to get better when no one could help him. He never slept well, but cried all night, "Please help me, Nan. Lorn, I'm so sick. Mommy, I need something to eat." We were helpless to do anything but weep with him.

Having to work in the fields and come home to take care of everyone was really hard work. Phanny and I were both feeling weak and sick with fever, and Heng had no control over his bowels. When the infection became especially bad, each of us had only a combination of blood and mucous from our bowels, and the smell was overwhelming. Phanny and I cleaned this from Heng's body many times a day.

It was a long walk to the place where we could wash clothes, so in order to reserve my strength, I began having Heng sleep naked. This was uncomfortable for him because the board on which he was sleeping had splinters in it and his bony little body could not really rest.

I will never forget the last day Heng was alive. When I woke up that morning, I felt both tired and dizzy, but I had to go to the field so we could get some rice that noon. Before I left, Heng begged, "Please, Lorn, let me sleep with the blanket under my body today."

The thought of having to come back that night and take the blanket to wash it again was more than I could take, so I refused him. Again he asked with tears in his eyes, but I still told him he could not have it. I went off to the field and when I returned at midday, Heng begged, "Please give me the blanket for a little while. I will die soon and I would like to have it under my body when I die. Then I will not cause you any more trouble." Trying not to hear his sobs, I turned and left the house without giving him what he so desperately wanted.

That night I came home to find that Heng had died. Mother said that he woke up in the middle of the afternoon, saying, "Mommy, Houng talked to me again. I hope when I die I can be with him or someplace like America or France. I do not want to return to live in Cambodia."

You see, my family was Buddhist and believed traditionally in life after death that is lived out here on earth. Heng had lost all hope and will to live, but even at the end of his young life, he knew that he did not want to return to Cambodia.

As I prepared Heng's body for burial, I felt very guilty. I could have made him happy in his last hours, but I had failed him. I cried as I put clean clothes on Heng and wrapped his body. I held him close. I knew that he could not hear me, but I had to whisper, "Sweet Heng. You are my special little brother and I love you very much. I am sorry you had to suffer so much. I will remember you always."

I felt so weak and did not know how to cope with the unbelievable problems we faced. Again Phanny and I went together to bury another of our loved ones. As we put his body in the grave, I felt as though a part of myself were being put there.

By the first of October 1976, just a few weeks after Phanny and I returned to live with the family, we had lost Father and three brothers. Following each death there were the tears of a heartbroken family, but there was also a kind of relief that the loved one would no longer suffer, that we would no longer have to hear their painful cries in the night. It's hard to describe how totally exhausted, both emotionally and physically, I felt at this point. I still desperately wished that God would allow us to die together rather than have to face the torture of wondering who would die next and how it would happen. I knew, though, that God wanted me to continue to function. He was giving me the promised strength beyond human understanding.

Each time we had to bury one of our loved ones, the task became more difficult. I felt that maybe I should stay near the grave after the burial. Two of my father's kind old friends had helped with each of these sad experiences and when I hesitated leaving Heng's grave, one man said, "You have been a good girl and done all you can. Now you must go rest so you can take care of the rest of the family." My unspoken cry was, *But how? Don't you see that I cannot take care of them? I am weak. There is no one to give me advice. My family is all dying and I don't know what to do!* I didn't put those thoughts into words because I did not want to hear them myself. We had a very difficult situation, but when I looked around at the other people in the village, I felt sad because everyone was facing major hurts and heartbreak. Sometimes the leader would wait several days before sending someone to help a family bury one of their loved ones. Not only was it emotionally difficult to have the body remain in the house that long, but it caused physical problems for everyone in the area. The stench sometimes became so bad that even people in other houses would become very ill. If there was anything in our stomachs, we would vomit, but usually we could not even do that. That smell, combined with the pangs of starvation and the deplorable living conditions, continued to add to the death toll. Sometimes I wondered how many had died and if this was what was happening all over Cambodia. It was so senseless, and I knew that we would all be dead very soon.

Phanny felt that too. I remember one day when we were taking food from the central kitchen to Mother, Nan, and Mouy Xea. Phanny was only fifteen, but very mature for her years. As we walked to the house from the kitchen, Phanny thought out loud, "I wonder how we will die, Lorn. Everyone around is dying, and it cannot be over until we are all dead. How do you think we will die?" I hadn't even thought about Phanny's dying, and my throat felt very tight when I heard her words. I couldn't even answer her, but felt a little more alone. Somehow the responsibility seemed to become heavier.

The cruelties of the Khmer Rouge never let up. When the soldiers came by and saw that Nan, who had been very sick, felt a little better and could walk, though slowly, they forced her to go back to work. She told them, "Even though I can walk a little, I still feel very weak and dizzy." They responded, "If you can walk, you can work. Otherwise you are lazy. That is a crime requiring great punishment."

So Nan went back to work in the fields. This was hard on her as well as on the baby. He loved her so much and did not like being left with the old woman who took care of the children. When Nan went to get the baby at night, he recognized her immediately and smiled, even though he was very weak. Nan had never had enough milk to breast-feed the baby. Since his birth, we had only been able to give him a little amount of the rice we received mixed with a lot of water to make a cereal. We were never able to give him enough to make him a strong, happy baby.

Conversation was scarce, but everything we did hear was centered around someone's death. Because we had lost most of our family, everyone even remotely related became important to us. We were saddened to learn that Nan's sister-in-law and our cousin had died at about the same time as Father. Though they were living in different villages and we hadn't seen them since before coming to the forest, the news added to the weight of the burden we carried.

Since the day Father died, Phanny and I had taken turns sleeping next to Mother to help her during the night. Worried about her, I slept very lightly and probably only two or three hours a night. Her touch on my leg was our signal that she could stand the pain no longer. When she did this, I knew that she must feel very sick, because she would not "bother" me until it was absolutely necessary. She knew how limited my strength was. I hope she knew how deep my love was.

Sometimes I lay awake beside her, thinking of happy times. The hours I had spent watching her cooking and sewing, the times I had come home late at night to find her waiting up for me—all were expressions of her deep and lasting love. I desperately wanted to give back some of that love, so I did all I could to ease her pain.

This usually meant getting up at least ten times each night to keep the draining, infected wounds clean. I would wipe her fevered body, put fresh water on her dry lips and into her mouth, and wash her body if she lost control of her bowels. The nauseating smell of her illness often woke us several times a night, sometimes even making us sick, though we usually could not even vomit.

It hurt deeply to see Mother so sick. Part of her suffering was having to be so completely dependent on us, her children. Mother wanted to help us and to live as long as we did. She knew, though, that she was often delirious and incoherent. One day she told me to take a little piece of the gold we had left and buy some medicine. She was hoping it would renew her strength and heal her body. For that gold I bought twenty aspirin on the black market. They had no healing power, but they did ease her pain for a while. I kept ten of the pills for Mother and sold the others to a neighbor. I made a small profit, so did something to protect our future.

Nan had become very sick again and stayed home with Mother. In early November my legs began to swell to a very large size. I could not walk on them, so I, too, had to stay home. Because it was the rainy season, our thatched roof was leaking and everything in the house was always wet. My resistance was so low that I got malaria very badly and became extremely weak. My eyes were yellow and I was always cold. One time I was sleeping and dreamed I had twenty blankets on top of me but was still cold. Phanny made herb medicine for me, but it did not help.

Phanny and Tak were the strong ones now. They had to bring food to us all. Sometimes Tak would wander off to the central kitchen by himself and return with stories of how much the soldiers were eating. Sometimes he would say, "They cooked the beef with the rice and it smelled so good. The vegetables they were eating were so beautiful. I could almost taste them." When I had the strength, I got very angry at him for this. His comments made me realize my helplessness again.

Mother had taken all of the aspirin, without a noticeable change in her health. Phanny was able to get combinations of roots and leaves that were supposed to help take the infection away, but nothing worked. One day Mother realized that unless she immediately took a more effective medication, she would die. There was no other hope.

As we talked about it, we thought of Kuon, a man who lived across the river. He was a good, friendly man. We were sure he would give some of his medicine to us if he knew that Mother needed it. Phanny was feeling the strongest, so Mother asked her to go quickly and beg Kuon for his help.

We knew that it had been raining but didn't realize how much rain had fallen or how high the river would be. Usually we could wade across the river, but now I realize that when Phanny ventured into the water, she knew she could not possibly get to the other side on her own. I also know that she would not have been able to bear returning to face us without the medicine Mother needed. We knew that Mother would die without it, but we had not wanted to consider the possibility that she might even die after taking the medicine. We didn't want to think about it.

Nan and I were sitting outside our house about a half-hour after Phanny had left. As Mother slept inside, we talked in low voices. Nan was saying, "I hope it doesn't take too long for this medicine to work. Mother is so tired of not being able to go outside. She wants to be independent again."

The cook liked Phanny, and we were not surprised to

see her walking toward us. I called to her, "Phanny is not here. She's gone to get medicine for Mother." The cook looked almost sympathetic as she said, "Phanny has drowned in the river. She will not come back to you. One of the men saw her being carried away by the big waves."

It seemed like someone else talking when I heard my voice saying, "But she was just here. You can't mean that. She's strong and good. No one can take my hope, my Phanny, from me. Please tell me you could be talking about someone else."

The cook just turned and walked toward the river. I took a stick that Tak had found. I used it to help me hobble around. As I walked, I tried to keep up with the cook. The distance to the river was more than a kilometer and I felt as though I was walking on stumps, but I had to see for myself what had happened to my baby sister.

When I got to the river, I was amazed to see how high and gushing it was. As if in a dream, I heard the cook tell a soldier, "Search down the side of the river to see if you can find the body of Phanny." After looking for a short while and finding nothing, he came back and said, "The river is moving so quickly that her body is surely far downstream by this time. We will never find it." I couldn't believe what I was hearing. It had happened: Phanny had died.

Before the death of my other family members I had at least been able to console them. I had the chance to show my love to them. But for the one whom I loved in such a special way, I had not even been able to say, "Good-bye, my sweet sister. I love you." I knew that shouting it would do no good, but I felt like shouting. I also wanted to scream at someone, "Stop this, I'm not able to take any more of this pain. You must stop now." But I couldn't shout. I couldn't even sit down to rest. I had to go home. The rest of the family was waiting for me. The cook went quickly ahead as I made my way slowly back to the house. I felt that I was going from one painful experience to another. The emptiness in my heart hurt.

As I walked, I cursed that river, remembering it was the same one Father, Hy, and I had first worked on when we arrived in the forest in 1975. I had felt bad when many people had suffocated under falling dirt as we dug the riverbed. Now it had taken my baby sister from me. She hadn't even been sick. She shouldn't be dead, but there was no one to punish for the injustice. *Why, God, why?* I wondered, and remember thinking I was certainly going to go crazy now. I didn't care. Not even survival mattered.

Soon after I arrived home, a friend of Kuon's came to see me. I was amazed when he said, "Kuon and I were on the other side of the river when Phanny went into the water. It was moving so fast that we were sure she could swim or she wouldn't have tried to cross. We were shocked when she got to the middle of the river and saw her hands go in the air and her beautiful long black hair flying behind her as the waves beat against her body and soon swept her away. It all happened so quickly that even though I'm a strong swimmer, I knew I would not be able to save her life. I'm so sorry."

Phanny was no longer ours to love. Now Mother had lost her favorite child. We had always known and accepted her as special to Mother. It was my responsibility to relay the bad news.

117

Before I could get inside the house, Mother was calling for me. Though I thought she was sleeping, Mother had heard the cook tell us about Phanny's death hours ago. Since then, she had been all by herself, weeping over the tragic loss of her fifteen-year-old baby girl. Although she knew what had happened, Mother wanted to hear every detail. As I relayed them to her, she sobbed. Her thin, weak body shook as she screamed, "My baby. My dear Phanny died while trying to save my life. But I cannot live without my baby!"

7

The Loneliness of Aloneness

Hy's weakness made me afraid to tell him about the other members of our family. (At the time he had been forced to leave us, only Houng had died.) When we settled down, he looked around the room. Realizing that the four of us were alone, he asked, "Is the rest of the family in the fields?" I gently said, "No, Hy. Everyone else has died. The four of us are alone."

None of us could get to sleep that night. Mother tossed and turned all night, mumbling in her delirium. As I tried to rest beside her, I thought about Phanny and how much I loved her. She had always been so strong, loving, and helpful. I knew I would miss her terribly as a friend, and I didn't know how we would get along without her help in taking care of us all.

The anguish in Mother's voice and eyes as she called Nan and me to her side the next day made me realize that I would have to find a way to fill the place in her life left empty by Phanny's death. As I watched her painstakingly force her thoughts into words, I knew as never before how dearly I loved my mother and how meaningful the years were that we had spent together. If only there were a way to bring a smile to her lips.

She begged, "Please work very hard to take care of everything the way Phanny did. Be sure that Tak stays well. *Love each other.*"

As a young girl with lots of changing emotions, I was sure I had often disappointed my mother. Because Phanny was still very young, she was like a child to Mother; they had never experienced any major disagreements, so Mother saw her as perfection. I felt sorry for the times I had hurt Mother, but didn't know how I could convince her that I wanted to do all she had asked and much more. I wanted to be perfect for her but could only continue lying by her side every night to help her, secretly eating less so that I could give her more.

Because the infection in my feet and legs had made them swollen, it was still very hard to walk, but with great pain I went to the central kitchen each day with Tak. We would beg the cook for extra food. When she gave it to me, I became angry, wondering why she had not done this while my family was alive and well enough to benefit from the sugar and rice that was there and available. Now Mother was so weak she could hardly even swallow anything. I knew the cook had taken a risk in giving me these extras, and I appreciated that, but I desperately wished she had done so weeks earlier.

I could barely walk and Nan could not walk at all, so it was up to little Tak to carry the water to us. It was heavy, but he had stayed quite strong and his sweet spirit was encouraging.

Because I was so weak and Mother was so sick, it was very difficult to help her, especially in the dark of the night. With some fear, I asked the leader for a lamp so I could see at night rather than having to "see" with my hands. I wanted the light so I could watch Mother's face at night. Now she was often too weak to even touch my leg to let me know she needed me.

The leader gave me a tiny lamp and told me to use it only when absolutely necessary. She said, "Do not leave it on all night or you will waste too much oil." I accepted the lamp and took it to our house and told Nan indignantly, "I cannot believe she would tell me not to 'waste oil' on Mother. She is dying, and that woman is worried about a little oil!" But I was glad to have the lamp.

Each day following Phanny's drowning, Mother talked less. When she did want to say something, it was usually to mourn Phanny's death. She wept often, saying, "I am so sorry I asked Phanny to go after medicine for me. She gave up any chance for a full life to die for me. I am an old woman. I should have been the one to die, not Phanny." When I heard Mother say that, I could stand it no longer. I crawled slowly down the steps to the ground. There I sat weeping when a soldier came by. He knew that Mother was sick, but he did not care. In fact, he laughed saying, "It is better for her to die than a cow. The cows are good. They help us a lot and do not eat rice. They are much better than you pigs!"

I was afraid to argue with him because I knew he would surely have me killed. It was dangerous enough that he had seen me show my "weakness" by crying. I was thankful when he walked on by me, but I wished there were a way to hurt him as he had hurt me.

Within three days after Phanny drowned, Mother was eating almost nothing. The night of the fourth day, I woke up beside her, knowing it would be our last night like this. I looked at her face in the dim lamplight and knew that I wouldn't feel her hand on my leg, hear her voice, or ever be able to help her again. I would only wash her body one more time—as I prepared her for burial. My grief was so overwhelming when I realized she had died that at first I could not even weep.

I turned the lamp off and held her hand the rest of the night, trying unsuccessfully to keep it warm. I cannot describe how intensely sad and lonely I felt. I didn't know why I should continue to live, or what purpose there was in enduring the constant suffering to which I woke up every morning.

With each death I had faced in the last months, I

thought the pain could never be worse. Now I realized that the pain was different with each death because my relationship with each family member was different. I thought of all these things during those hours after Mother's last breath, but knew I would have to regain my strength for Nan and Tak. I would have to make the arrangements for my mother's burial.

I drifted off to sleep and woke up without opening my eyes the next morning. I desperately wished it had been a bad dream, but the coldness of Mother's hand in mine convinced me the most dreaded day had arrived. First I had to tell Nan that our Mother had died.

Before I could do that, I saw her weeping. Mouy Xea was in her arms. I suddenly realized that he, too, had died during the night. Nan sobbed as she told me that just before he died she was awakened by his movement and saw him crying, but he was so weak there was no sound coming from him. She could see him in the dim lamplight and realized that he was trying to get his breath. He could not, however, and at that moment he died. Nan had spent the rest of the night mourning her baby and the fact that Meng had never seen their baby's face.

Now there were three of us. Nan and I knew that before we could give in to our grief we had to arrange for the burial of the baby and our mother. We longed for a stronger person on whom we could lean, but there was no one. I wished that Hy were near. There was no way to verify it, but we had heard that he, too, had died. We were alone in our loneliness. I remembered again that God had given Jesus up to death because He loved me. He must understand how I felt losing the one I loved most. I wondered if He understood why I hated that soldier who was happy that Mother rather than one of his cows was dying.

I had arrangements to make. Our leader informed me that an old man had died the same night as Mother and the baby, so the three of them would be buried together because there was not enough empty space for separate graves. Besides, there was no reason to dig two when one was enough, they decided.

With trembling hands, I dressed Mother's body for the last time. I took the finest things we had. Nan did the same for the baby. When it was time to go to the gravesite, Nan wept. "I am too weak to even go to the burial of my own mother and baby. It is not fair!"

I carried the baby's body, hobbling slowly behind the two men who carried Mother, her hands and legs tied to a stick, as two others had carried Father to his grave. The old man, whom we didn't even know, was picked up and brought along to complete our procession. Tak was walking beside me, trying to help me walk because he knew I was in great pain.

Because it had been raining so much, it was difficult to find a burial place that was not covered with water. Finally we found a small area. I held the baby as the men placed Mother and the old man on the ground while they dug the hole. Khmer Rouge soldiers stood by and watched, showing no emotion. If they felt anything when one of us died, it was happiness. It did not take long to dig the shallow grave, but as I watched, I prayed with my eyes open. Anything else would have been very dangerous, but I needed God's strength as never before and knew that He understood my fear and loneliness.

The hardest part was to remain silent while they

placed Mother's body next to that of an old man she had never even seen. After the men had put her body down, I put Nan's baby in her arms, trying to stay calm in spite of the deplorable, sneering soldiers. The muddy dirt was being put on top of the body of my beloved mother. I heard the sounds of it falling, "plop, plop," but could no longer look. When they were finished, I grabbed Tak's hand and turned around and ran, momentarily unmindful of the pain shooting up my legs. I didn't know where I was going but, blinded by tears, knew I had to get away from those hateful men and the place where I had allowed them to put Mother's body next to someone other than Father.

Nan, Tak, and I continued to live, but actually, we were nearly dead. Neither Nan nor I could walk very well, so we could not go to work and were only given part of a can of rice each day—barely enough to exist.

Even for that little bit, we had to go to the central kitchen and fill out a form each day. In early November 1976, I was in the middle of this process when someone secretly told me he had heard that Hy was still alive. I was elated. Hy was alive! Now I would have someone to depend on again.

Forgetting to even go to the house to tell Nan and Tak where I was going, I began the long walk to the village where I was told I would find Hy in a hospital. It hurt so much to walk that I had to stop and rest often. When I finally reached the place where he was—ten kilometers from our house—I recognized his face immediately but was shocked to see his shrunken body.

He looked as small as one of the little boys. He was no longer my big strong brother. Now I would have to be strong for him, too. Again my expectations and hopes were shattered and my aloneness intensified. This excuse for a hospital was simply a shack with a thatched roof. I had heard that they were only places for people to go to die, and I was very angry to see Hy lying in front of it because there was not enough room inside. I looked in the door and saw several hundred people, all very near death. The nurses were not trained for the work. They were simply people chosen from among the "prisoners of war." One of the "nurses" told me that Hy had been lying outside the shack both day and night— in the cold and heat—for more than a week.

As I looked around, I knew I could not leave him there. He must return to our house with me. I knew he would never get any better in this place. I tried to regain my composure as I looked at him from several feet away. It had been raining only minutes before, so his wet shirt and short pants clung to him, and mosquitoes were swarming all over his scantily clad body, which was already full of bites. I wondered what horrors he had experienced, because it was evident that he had suffered many cruelties.

I went to his side and he opened his eyes at the sound of my voice, crying loudly, "Lorn, Christ has come to me. I saw Him. Christ came to me."

In his delirium, Hy did not realize that he was placing both our lives in danger by saying this for everyone to hear, so I tried to quiet him by whispering softly in his ear. I assured him, "I am here now. I will take care of you, Hy. You will not be treated cruelly any longer." He smelled so bad that I could hardly bear to hold his body in my arms—but he was my brother. He needed me.

I told the nurses that I wanted to take him home with me. They reminded me that Hy would not get his rice allotment unless he was at the hospital where he was registered. That could not stop me. I would find a way to get rice for him. So it was that we two—both very sick—began the long walk to our village. Hy was so much weaker than I that I had to help him walk. It was only on the way back home that I realized I had not told Nan where I was going and how worried she would be before we saw her again.

It was such a long walk that we had to stop to sleep one night. We had no food, but I found bitter-tasting forest fruit to eat. By the time we arrived at her bedside, Nan had spent many frightened hours worrying and weeping, certain I had been killed. She and Tak were both very shocked to see Hy with me. We were all excited to be together and we cried and cried. Hy's weakness made me afraid to tell him about the other members of our family. (At the time he had been forced to leave us, only Houng had died.) When we settled down, he looked around the room, Realizing that the four of us were alone, he asked, "Is the rest of the family in the fields?" I gently said, "No, Hy. Everyone else has died. The four of us are alone."

The shock of learning at one time that our parents, the boys, Phanny, and the baby had all died was so great that he would not believe it. For days Hy acted as though everyone was just away and would soon come back. He was totally irrational and laughed and sang most of the time, making me very afraid that the spies would become angry and we would be reported, but that never happened.

Whenever I had the chance to talk to Hy, I would try to find out what had happened to him. He had blocked the experiences from his mind and would not talk about

128

them. I was sure the torture must have been great, because his mind was severely affected. I would never again know the brother I remembered. His combination of weaknesses made it impossible for him to work, so I was the only one able to earn rice. We had very little to eat and were all becoming weaker by the day, but Hy suffered the most.

It was around this time that the truly unbelievable thing happened. The Khmer Rouge announced that they had enough rice that day and we could all eat until we were no longer hungry! For most of us this was like strong medicine from heaven. We felt as though we had new power and strength in our bodies. People smiled and talked for the first time in many months.

The extra food had a very strange effect on Hy. He began acting crazier than ever. The shock of having a full stomach must have been too much for him. He came to me, laughing, crying, and singing all at the same time. I was very frightened because I did not know what to say or how to help him. None of the rest of my family had had this kind of sickness. After several hours he quieted down, but I was afraid of what he might do or say next.

About mid-November the leader decided I was strong enough to work. I was sent away again from my loved ones. There were some people in the new place who knew me and had relatives in the village where Nan, Tak, and Hy were living. They were kind to me and relayed news as they heard it. Once again I was living in my hammock-home under a tree. I worried about the others. In their cruelty, the Khmer Rouge had forced Nan and Tak to move away from Hy, so he was alone except for the times Nan sent Tak to take him a little bit of rice and water and to check on him. Hy was delirious all the time now and he seldom even understood who we were. The Khmer Rouge regime was just too severe. They had no sympathy for anyone, regardless of how sick one was. Many people died because of the mind-crippling terror of the regime, and I believe that was the basic cause of Hy's sickness. I thought about this as I worked and as I tried to sleep in the hammock, but there was nothing I could do to fight back except to keep on surviving.

One day, less than a week after I had moved, someone told me that Hy had died. I ran all the way home, crying as I went and wishing I had been with him when he died. When I reached Nan's bed, she said that Tak had gone to see Hy and came back, crying, "Hy has died. I cannot wake him. Hy lives no more." Though it was extremely painful, Nan could walk very slowly with the support of an old stick, and she had gone to see Hy for herself. She could hardly believe it, but it seemed that Hy had gotten even smaller since the soldiers had forced her to move away from him a few days before.

Though very weak, Hy was not yet dead. He opened his eyes, trying very hard to say something to Nan. She painfully got down on her knees so she could put her ear to his mouth and hear him. "Please tell Lorn," he cried, "that I wish I could have seen her face one more time. I know she would have brought me something to eat so I would not have to die with an empty stomach." Those were his last words, and by the time I arrived home, one of the other refugees had buried my brother. My emotions were too raw by that time to be able to describe them with words.

I had left my New Testament and a few pieces of

clothing with Nan when I went to the new place. I decided to risk taking the New Testament back with me. I was surprised to find it missing. Nan said she had not even realized I had left it there, so she did not know where it could be. We were both frightened that one of the Khmer Rouge must have taken it, so we would surely be reported and killed immediately. I stayed overnight with Nan before leaving the next day and fully expected the soldiers to come for me, or for all of us, but they never did. God protected us. I pray that He used His Word to speak to the heart of the person who stole it.

The effects of the slow starvation we were experiencing continued. There were many days that we were so hungry we ate rice and vegetables raw from the field, leaves from the trees, or anything else we could find that was not poisonous. Like animals, we ate using only our mouths to lap up food. We did not have the luxury of considering what the "food" was doing to our stomachs, teeth, or health in general. We only knew that something in the stomach is necessary if one is to go on living.

Because Nan was so sick, I asked for permission to live with her. It was granted, but again with the understanding that my ration of rice would be cut in return for the privilege.

When I had the strength, I allowed myself to become very angry. It was hard to forgive, and I often wished I had a gun to return at least some of the hurt these people were inflicting on my loved ones. I had no gun, but Jesus was with me. He continued to reveal Himself at unexpected moments, giving me the will to continue and the assurance that He would never leave me. In my heart I knew that I could help my family and my God more by loving my enemy—the Khmer Rouge—than by hating them. So I asked Jesus to love them through me, even though I didn't really want to love them.

When I returned to our village, our leader told me I would have to take Tak to the "school" again. Nan and I were very sad to see him go, but most parents were having to do this, so we saw no alternative. It was only after several weeks' time that I began hearing stories about these "schools" and became frightened for Tak.

I was told the children did not get any medicine or their fair share of food. When a child was sick, or even when he died, parents were not informed. Getting permission to visit the school was very difficult, and people who went without permission were often put into the prison when they returned. This prison, I heard, had no doors. The people slept on the dirt without any roof over their heads—even during the monsoon season when the rain beat down on them. They received only a little bit of gruel every two or three days.

Whether in or out of prison, if a soldier decided a person needed punishment, there was no way to appeal it. The beatings they gave with a whip or board were cruel and became more brutal if the person protested. Sometimes the Khmer Rouge *children* gave these beatings—to men, women, and children of all ages. The damaging psychological effect of a child giving such punishment to an adult was very deep.

Everyone who disagreed with the Revolution in any way or indicated that he did not want to be a part of the society could very easily be shot. We were told that "the

Photo by E. Mooneyham

World Vision Hospital and staff in 1974

law of Kampuchea is at the end of a gun barrel." There was no doubt that they enforced it with great joy.

All in all, it was very unwise to go against the orders of the Khmer Rouge. But when I heard that the "school" to which I had taken Tak was very much like the "hospital" from which I had rescued Hy, I knew that I had to go after my little baby brother. As I walked toward the school, I thought about Hy. Perhaps he would still be alive if I had gotten to him earlier and taken him out of that hospital before he became so sick.

Anyway, I had told Mother that I would take care of Tak, and that was one promise I was going to keep. I managed to get to the school, into the part where Tak was sleeping, and back to our house—all in the same night. We were very hungry but managed to get by on our little bit of rice. Tak was frightened. The people at

133

the school had been so mean to him that the thought of being found and having to return was more than his seven-year-old mind could take. I assured him that no one could take him from me. "I'll take care of you always," I promised.

Several days later one of the spies heard Tak talking and reported his presence to our leader. She came to me and threatened to take away my rice allotment totally if I did not return Tak to the school. I knew there was no way any of us would live if we did not have some food from the central kitchen. The Khmer Rouge were very angry with me for defying their orders and taking Tak from the school, so would accept nothing less than for me to return him to that wretched place. Our neighbors were surprised that we had not both been killed immediately. I knew God was protecting me, but I wanted to protect Tak from them!

As we walked back down that long road, Tak and I both cried. He and Nan had had another tear-filled farewell and I was desperately trying to think of a way to save him from the hands of the soldiers. Poor Tak. Having been born in Phnom Penh, he had known war all his life. I wished he could have experienced some of our happy days in Ang Tasaom, so that he would have those memories.

Now, even though he was only seven years old, he was a prisoner of war, left to live with whatever torture the Khmer Rouge decided to give him. There was no one to protect him from the evil of these people. They did not care how old or young one was, they only wanted to destroy everyone in the most painful way possible. I was totally helpless to do anything for my last brother.

It was with these thoughts that in July 1977, I took him back inside the dirty, ugly "school." I held him close, telling him that I loved him, then I turned to walk quickly away. As I walked, I heard his sobbing voice call my name. I had to walk faster to get away from the sound of his voice.

It was less than a week later that I was on my way home from the field and someone quietly told me they had heard that little Tak was very sick. I could not endure being away from him, allowing him to be both sick and alone. As I fled to the school to see Tak, I disregarded the fact that my leader would likely take my rice allotment from me and probably would punish me severely.

Tak was too weak to stand up and so thin that he was no longer cute. I looked at his face with its sharply-protruding bones, and his matchstick-like arms and legs. I somehow felt guilty that I had not been able to find a way to take care of him. I bent down next to him and whispered, "Tak, I am here. I will never leave you alone again." His eyes fluttered open, but he was too weak to talk. The look in his eyes told me, however, that he was relieved to see me. In that moment I saw some of the terror leave his little face and I felt him relax in my arms.

He had been thin before I had taken him back to the school—we all were—but now, like almost everyone, he had malaria, which had taken every bit of strength and look of good health from him. No one had helped him eat, so he had had nothing in his stomach for at least three days. Although I hated doing it, I took him to the local "hospital." As I feared, it was very much like the one from which I had taken Hy. I stayed there with him,

Close-up view of World Vision Hospital and staff in 1974

much against their rules, sleeping on the ground next to Tak, trying to love and take care of him. When I tried to feed him the gruel I was given, he would push my hand away. His stomach was so small that he could only take two or three bites, then would begin to vomit. I did what I could to make him comfortable, reminding him all the time of my love for him—and whispering of Jesus' love for him.

Like others in my family, his skin became transparent, his stomach swollen; and like the others, his bowel movements were a combination of blood and mucous. There were hundreds like him all around me. The effect of the sights and smells sometimes made me so ill that I had to leave his bedside to get fresh air.

Little Tak lived on at the "hospital" for more than a week. One night I felt him clutch my fingers and

136

whisper my name. He told me that he knew he was going to die. He woke me three other times that night, each time saying, "Lorn, please give me water."

Light was coming through the thatched roof after the third time, and I lay there watching him. His breathing was heavy and he was mumbling in his sleep. Several times I heard him say, "Mommy, Mommy." Soon after that call he became very peaceful, and when I sat up to look at him, I realized that he was no longer breathing. Little Tak had died and he would never again know the terror of war or the pain of hunger. Now Nan and I were alone.

I made arrangements to have Tak buried and took care of his body in the best way I could. Then I had to begin the long, lonely walk back to Nan by myself. Thankful that we had each other, we felt sure that we would die together. It was inevitable that we would die in just a matter of time. Since we knew, however, that it would be unbearable if one of us was left alone, we wanted to die at the same time. When we had talked about it, we realized that the only way to be sure we died at the same time was to plan it. We talked about the possibility of refusing to eat for several days. If we did that, it wouldn't take more than three or four days for us to die. When we talked about this, God seemed to say, *Don't you want to see what I'll do with your life? Don't you wonder why I have preserved and protected you for this long?* Of course we did. Even though Nan did not know Jesus, she felt there was a reason that we were still alive.

When I arrived at our house after the long walk from the "hospital," I told her how Tak had died. We wept together. Now we had to decide if we wanted to fight to survive or to give up and die together. We came to the conclusion that having survived this long, we wanted to show the Khmer Rouge that we were strong and could keep living, even under their regime. I also wanted to have as much time as possible to share God's love with Nan so that she, too, could know Him.

Finally we became strong enough that we could both go back to work. Though not very strong, we did manage to work to get the food we needed to stay alive. In one way, I was happy that our parents had not lived long enough to experience the extremes of the Khmer Rouge tortures. Even though I did not know them, it made me cry to see the way the soldiers beat old people who were too weak to work hard. There was no end to their insensitivity.

There were days that I felt very sick, but something always gave me the will to live. As I matured in my relationship with the Lord, He helped me understand that He had a purpose for my life—that there was a reason to stay alive for the tomorrows. He gave me the grace to be kind even to the Khmer Rouge. One day I realized that the soldiers had been *taught* to be cruel, and I wondered what they would have been like if they had known a different kind of life. I could feel God changing my attitudes, making me want to be kind and understanding of the soldiers.

As this happened day after day, I began to see something different in the eyes of some of the Khmer Rouge. They could not be openly kind to me, but sometimes I got a little extra rice or a little piece of fish that I knew were gifts from God.

Sometimes God actively used our neighbors to encourage us. I especially remember a woman who lived close by and shared with us the food her husband found in the forest, giving us the strength we needed for that particular day. If sick for more than three days, we were supposed to be severely punished for the crime of weakness, but I was sick much of the time in 1978, and miraculously, Nan was allowed to bring my regular portion of rice to me, and neither of us was punished. God *did* care. There were reasons to continue surviving.

While I was very ill, we were fortunate that Nan was well. My body became very swollen in the same way that Mother's and the boys' had been. I could not walk for many weeks. Nan tried many different mixtures of herbs, but none of them helped very much.

Using the toilet became an especially painful process because I was swollen so greatly, and Nan or someone else would have to help me balance myself and then lift me up to a standing position when I was finished. We had learned long before this that we could not have the luxury of pride but had to welcome every offer of help to stay alive. Nothing else was important.

As I passed in and out of my dreams in those days, I remember wondering if I would ever be a "lady" again, if there would ever be a time when I could take a hot bath, smell good, wear a dress and high-heeled shoes, laugh and talk with friends. Of course, that could never be. Looking at my large, swollen body, I felt sure that I would soon die with Nan, while still living in the denseness of the forest.

As the days moved on, the seasons changed and we became alternately desolate and hopeful. Just at the time when I thought the Khmer Rouge were becoming "softer," more human, I would hear another story that made me cry with anger. One of my neighbors told me about an old man she saw being forced to dig his own grave before they cut his throat. Nan came home from work one day and said that someone had known a young man who was heard complaining about the severe torture given his parents. Cuts were made all over his body and salt poured in them. The pain was so unbearable that he ran all the way to the river and took his own life by throwing himself into it. The Khmer Rouge said that he had done this because he did not feel worthy of being a part of the Revolution.

I believed that Satan was using his great strength to make the Khmer Rouge soldiers as cruel as possible. I was thankful that even though their cruelties had changed my life, God was stronger and the one ultimately in control!

One day while Nan and I were working in the fields, everyone was told to get into a large circle. Four people, two men and two women, then went around the circle, the women putting their hands inside our clothing and all over our bodies, looking for gold or any other valuables. The men did the same to the men in the circle. Nan was very smart. After they had searched her, she slipped away and ran home because we still had a little bit of gold hidden there. She raced up the stairs to get it and then back down to hide it under the dirt next to one of the posts on which our house was built. She was back in the fields before the soldiers arrived to search our house, and they did not find our last little bit of treasure.

Day after day we continued this sad life, wondering how it would end. My body was filled with calluses, but my hands, feet, and back had never become hardened to the strenuous work we were forced to do. Sometimes while working in the fields, I would watch the birds, envying their freedom. They could eat whatever they found, fly away whenever they wanted, or build a house in almost any spot that suited them.

We had no such freedom. We felt as though we were living in hell with no way out. The food we ate smelled terrible, was dirty, and probably had bugs in it, but it was something in our stomachs, so we accepted it. We were punished when we were sick, were treated worse than the animals, and laughed at if we showed emotion for a sick loved one.

Nan and I had trouble keeping track of the weeks and months as one melted into another. In early January 1979 we heard the rumor from one of our neighbors that the Vietnamese had invaded the northern part of Cambodia. "They are going to overthrow the Khmer Rouge," a neighbor said with excitement. She said that they would take over the country and be our new rulers.

We didn't know what it would be like to live under the Vietnamese rulers, but anything would be better than the terror-filled experiences of the last four years. It sounded like another hopeless dream to me, but I thought about it often in the days following and prayed that God would continue to guide us. In early April we began to hear far in the distance the sound of guns and rockets that had to be the guns of the Vietnamese. I began to believe that it was possible that someone might free us from this terrible existence under Pol Pot and his Khmer Rouge forces.

8

Those Who Didn't Die

The years in the forest, living under the cruel Khmer Rouge regime, had taught us to protect ourselves and never trust or believe the promises of others — especially anyone in authority. "Now," Nan said to me one evening, "we need to learn to trust others again."

The Khmer Rouge soldiers heard those machine guns, too, and wonder of wonders, they ran! I couldn't believe my eyes but I was so happy to see them running away from the village, to see them with fear in their eyes. Even though I knew it wasn't the best attitude, I said to Nan, "Maybe now they'll get what they deserve—someone stronger than they are."

All of us—their "prisoners of war"—ran, too. Nan and I went with Heang, a friend whose husband had been killed and whose three children had died from starvation. Heang had become another sister to us, and we loved her very much. Until we really knew what was happening, we wanted to stay near the central kitchen and water supply, so we only went a little way into the forest. There we hid, crouching near a tree, trying to make ourselves invisible. We heard the Khmer Rouge in the area and knew we would be shot at once if they saw us. We didn't know what a Vietnamese soldier would do, but we were afraid to find out. We stayed there for many hours before we dared to go back to the village to get a little rice and water. When we finally took the risk, it was with great fear of being caught and killed.

Several days later I was returning from the central kitchen to our hiding place, with my arms full of food, when I saw a Vietnamese soldier. We both froze. There was no place for me to hide. I was so frightened that words could not come. I thought I had lost my voice forever. Finally, he said "Pol Pot? Pol Pot?" He wondered if I was part of the Khmer Rouge people. Because I could not speak Vietnamese, I spoke in Khmer saying, "No, I am people. I am not Pol Pot. They have gone."

He followed me to the little hiding place we had been living in. Another of our people was hiding nearby and she recognized some of his Vietnamese words. Before Cambodia fell to the Khmer Rouge, she had been very proficient in the languages. Of course, she had blocked it from her mind to avoid the dangers. Now she could only recall a few words, but she could understand words the soldier said.

When he realized this, the soldier spoke very slowly, saying, "Stay close with your group of people. Don't scatter too much or too far away from the place. We know the Pol Pot soldiers are still in the area. If they see you, they will not have mercy on you."

For ten days we stayed in that place, going carefully to the central kitchen when necessary. One day I brought back more things than we needed, for we had decided that we would begin walking away. The Lord seemed to be telling me that it would be dangerous to stay much longer.

Before we left, I prayed that this would be our last such journey and that we would be walking toward freedom. We decided to go in the direction of Moung, about a three-day walk from our place in the forest. At the end of the first day, we stopped to rest for the night at a potato farm. While we were sitting there, some men with a tractor that was pulling an old cart came by us. They stopped to talk.

At first we were very frightened, but we soon realized that they were kind and did not want to hurt us or take advantage of us. They had come down to this area from Battambang City in the north and had picked rice and other food to sell in the market at Battambang City.

My eyes must have lit up when they said that, because one of them asked me if I knew someone in the city. I told him about my aunt and uncle who had once lived there. "I'm afraid they're probably not still alive," I said. He was very kind, though, and said, "Well, you might as well come with us and see if you can find them." I wanted to very much, but I was terribly afraid of what would happen if we had another dream cave in on us and I knew Nan had the same fear. My emotions were so tender, so raw.

But the man was convincing. So the three of us found a spot on the cart, and off we went. It took several hours to ride to the city, but very early in the trip I realized I felt happiness. We were driving away like free people— we could say whatever we wanted. I felt like one of the birds I had envied for four years.

When we stopped to eat, they asked if I could cook. I was anxious to see if I remembered. Making a meal for kind friends and feeling like a free woman was the greatest joy I could imagine. As we ate, we talked and laughed. Everyone seemed to realize that at least for that night we had to try to forget that the Pol Pot forces existed. We could be realistic later.

It was fun to talk to men again. For fear of being severely beaten and perhaps even put into prison, during the four years in the forest I had not had a conversation with a man who was not a relative. The only ones allowed to marry during those years were those ordered to do so by the soldiers. Usually those two people did not know each other and had no feelings of love.

Now God was healing those raw, hurting wounds. In this happy atmosphere it almost seemed that the memories were part of a story someone had told me. Then I remembered my family and knew it wasn't just a story.

We arrived in Battambang about 8:00 P.M. I was shocked at the sight of civilization. My eyes saw real buildings rather than the simple shacks we had known for so long. Light was shining from them. People were riding bicycles and motorbikes. I had almost forgotten about them. These people were all alive—really alive. Even though I saw it with my eyes, my mind could not comprehend it as reality. I kept wondering when the Khmer Rouge soldiers would appear and where we should go to find safety. *Surely*, I thought, *this bit of heaven couldn't last for long.*

When I expressed this to our friend, he explained, "The Vietnamese entered Battambang City several months ago. We have had this much freedom since then. Still, we must be careful. There's not too much to eat and it's almost impossible to leave this country, but we are not tortured as we were when Pol Pot had the power." I didn't see how anyone could ask for any better life than this. I even started to think again about the possibility of security rather than just survival.

The man driving the tractor asked if we wanted to stay at his house. He had been very kind but had many children and other relatives living with him, so we decided to accept the invitation of two men who had lost their wives to starvation and had a larger house with more space.

Going into their house, which I now realize was very

146

small, was like going into another world. They had furniture. And a place to cook. The beds were pieces of board, much like those we had known in the village, but they were not filled with splinters—and they were dry. The rain could not even get into the house.

It took a long time for me to get to sleep that night. I whispered to Nan, "I am afraid to sleep. I am afraid I will wake up with a Khmer Rouge soldier looking at me."

I finally did sleep, though. Waking up to remember that I was free seemed like a miracle. "Thank you, God," I said out loud so that anyone listening could hear it.

It felt so good to wash myself that morning. With deep joy I told Nan, "Watching the dust and dirt go off my body almost makes me feel like the experiences of the last four years are going away from me." We both sensed that there were problems ahead, but I knew that God would give us the strength we needed.

There was a small, cracked mirror in the house. Looking in it, I saw my face for the first time in four years. I was shocked to see how old and thin I looked. I was only twenty-five years old, but no one would have believed it. Nan said, "Maybe it would help if you had some of your makeup," but I didn't think even that makeup would make a difference. "It doesn't matter," I said. "We are alive and today we are going to search this city to see if we have relatives still alive."

Before we left our friends' house, we ate. Think of it! We could eat when we were hungry! Our friends were not wealthy and did not have a lot of food, but when they left they said, "Eat whatever you want. Enjoy it." We had become so accustomed to being treated cruelly that such kindness was hard to understand. We knew that we had to be careful not to eat too much or we would become sick, so with only a little bit in our stomachs, we left the house. Heang and I went to one busy area of town; Nan went relative-hunting in another direction.

Heang and I found a marketplace—just a small area where a few people were selling some rice, vegetables, and a few other things they were using to barter. Walking among them, I saw a lady selling *nom lout*— homemade rice cakes. I hadn't seen them in four years, but I could almost taste them from that far away. It was too bad that I didn't have something to sell. I would have enjoyed putting one into my mouth.

Battambang's market was nothing like the bustling one in which we had worked in Phnom Penh, but it brought back memories. I wished Father could be walking beside me. If only he and the rest of the family could have lived this long. As Heang and I walked on down the street, I looked closely at every single face. I'm sure some of the people thought I was strange, but if my family had changed as much as I had changed in the last four years, they would be very difficult to recognize.

"Lord," I cried, "I am very afraid of walking past them without knowing them. Please show my family to me." I so desperately wanted to find someone I could trust, someone who would hold me close and say, "Everything will be all right." Perhaps this was the reason God had not allowed me to die in the forest. Perhaps these family members were the reason I was still alive.

When it started to become dark, we decided to return to the house of our friend. I wanted to know if Nan had

had better success. We were walking past one particular side street when the Lord seemed to say, "Walk down that street." As we did, I looked in the window of a small house and saw my uncle's face. My aunt was standing behind him. "It's like seeing Mother," I whispered.

Without knowing or even thinking, I went to the door, threw it open, and ran to my aunt. She was very surprised, wondering who this girl could be. When I said, "I am Lorn. I am your sister's daughter," she took me in her arms and held me close. Soon the whole family was crowded around me. We laughed and cried. I couldn't find words to say how I felt, but I had found *family*. I had love and security once more. These were people who had not died under Pol Pot.

Somehow I had to find words to respond to their questions about Mother, Father, and the children. "Everyone has died," I sobbed. "Mother, Father, the boys, Phanny, and Nan's baby. Only Nan and I have survived to come to you." When they heard this sad news, we all held each other close and cried. This was the first time I was really able to grieve over the deaths of my loved ones. For many minutes we just stood together holding each other and wiping our tears.

Suddenly we realized that Nan was not with us. I knew she would be worried and of course the family truly wanted so much to see her again. So Heang and I returned to the other side of town to get her. As we left, my aunt cautioned, "Please be careful!" I think she was afraid to let me out of her sight. It felt good to have someone protecting me again.

Even though our feet hurt, we ran. I could hardly wait to tell Nan the exciting news. I knew she wouldn't be able to believe it until she saw the family, but I was anxious to see her eyes when I said, "We are no longer alone in the world. Our aunt and uncle live." Having family again seemed even more wonderful than the promise of freedom.

Finally Heang and I reached the house. I ran in, shouting, "Nan, I found them. They live and want us to come to them. You will love them. They want to see you now." It was a shock to her. Because she couldn't believe it, I wanted to show these newfound relatives to her. We invited Heang to join us, but she declined, saying that she had accepted an invitation to live with our two friends as their cook and housekeeper. I was sorry to leave Heang. We had experienced so much together, but I accepted her decision. We thanked our friends for their friendship and hospitality, then we hurriedly returned "home."

It was a joyful reunion that I will always remember. My aunt had fixed food while I was gone to get Nan. Just like Mother, she had made some of the traditional Cambodian favorites. While we heard their experiences and they heard ours, Nan and I ate chicken with vegetables and good rice. These were things I thought I would never even see or smell again. For dessert, we had *nom lout*—rice cakes like those I had seen in the market that afternoon. "I didn't know I would ever be this happy again," I told my uncle as I sat close to him.

It was with a great sigh of relief that I went to sleep that night. Finally a great dream had become reality. I felt secure. I had family around me, enough good food in my stomach, and a warm dry place in which to rest. We were treated so beautifully that it was an adjustment to shed the animal-like behavior we had adopted so long ago, but we would learn. Life was peaceful once again.

Even though there were fourteen people in my aunt's family, she accepted Nan and me as her own. I knew that she would do all she could to love and care for us. After two or three days of rest, I became anxious to help. I began working with my uncle.

Every day he went out to gather food from nearby farms to sell at a small market on the street outside their house. He also had a little bit of gold, which, along with the different kinds of food and some things my aunt made in her kitchen, he used to barter with the people. Working was now a joy, not something I was terrorized into doing from dawn till dark.

The years in the forest, living under the cruel Khmer Rouge regime, had taught us to protect ourselves and never to trust or believe the promises of others—especially anyone in authority. "Now," Nan said to me one evening, "we need to learn to trust others again."

Each day at my aunt's house, I felt myself becoming stronger. I was gaining weight. Every night we had bacon, chicken, or fish, and all the rice we could eat. I was beginning to feel like a young lady rather than an old worn-out woman. Life was fun.

About two weeks after our arrival in Battambang, I was surprised very early one morning to see many people walking together through the town. I started walking alongside one lady and asked where everyone was going. She said, "We are headed toward Thailand. We are very afraid that the Vietnamese government will not be in power very long. We must escape before the cruel Khmer Rouge rule again." I learned they had a guide who would take them to the Thailand-Cambodian border. "Another group will be going soon," she said and gave me the name of someone I could see to ask for more details.

When I went to see this man, he said, "Each group of three people must give me an ounce of gold, and it takes three days to walk through the forest to the border area. If you want to go, be here tomorrow morning at dawn. That is when we will leave."

I returned home, very excited about the possibilities. "Think of it," I said to my uncle, "we can walk toward certain freedom. There are more than two hundred people in his group. So many people would not be going if it were not safe. We will be a small number among those hundreds." This was the argument that won my uncle over to the plan. He and my aunt had a comfortable life in Battambang City and did not see a great reason for leaving there. "But," he reasoned to my aunt, "if we can have the freedom of a non-communist government and life together as a family, I think it is worth giving up this house." I would not have had enough gold for Nan and me to be part of the guide's group if my uncle had not helped. He was a generous man and had taken us as part of his own family. I knew he loved us.

It was on the afternoon of May 14, 1979, that we began the walk from Battambang to Thailand. It had been four years and a month since we had been forced to leave Phnom Penh and walk to Takeo. I thanked God for the differences between this walk and the other. To Nan I said, "Now we have every reason to be confident. I know we are headed toward freedom." I prayed as I walked.

It was a long, hard walk. The rains were very heavy,

so the mud was deep, and the large group moved very slowly. Because of the water everywhere on the ground, it was impossible even to sit down. At night we squatted, leaning against a tree to try to sleep. We would eat before beginning to walk in the morning and then again about midday. To keep the children quiet as we walked, we had bits of food ready to give to them.

This was a very dangerous walk because the Khmer Rouge soldiers were hiding out in the very forest through which we were walking. The guide told us, "The Khmer Rouge have set land mines to kill such groups as ours. You must walk very carefully." He didn't tell us that usually at least half of the people in each group died on the way. Again I prayed for God's guidance, reminding myself that He had been my protection during the last four years. For this journey I claimed that beautiful verse, "I will never leave thee nor forsake thee."

It was difficult to walk in the dense forest. We still didn't have shoes, so our feet were bleeding from stepping on plants with sharp edges. The smell of death was constantly around us, and we often saw human skeletons. The heavy rains made all of us sick, especially my aunt and uncle. Every time one of them coughed, I was afraid a Khmer Rouge soldier would hear it and come for us.

On the morning of the third day, the guide told us we would reach Thailand that day. That was exciting news, which made it easier to walk even though we all felt very ill from the strenuous hours of moving through the jungle. Several hours later, I heard him giving instructions for the rest of the trip. That's when I realized he wouldn't be with us. As if in the distance, I heard him

153

say, "Be very careful. Before you reach Thailand, you will have to run through an area where I know the Khmer Rouge soldiers are hiding. If they see you, they will kill you. Also, remember the possibility of land mines."

I could not believe my ears. *Why, God? Why would You let him bring us this far to abandon us? Please don't allow my family to die.*

Somehow I forced my legs to carry me across those last few kilometers. Everyone else found the strength and courage, too. We were frightened, and we ran as much of the time as our strength would allow. The mud was deep, forcing us to walk most of the time. Even though my legs were so weak I was afraid they might collapse, I knew that I had to help my aunt or she would have no hope of making it. We had almost run out of food and water, and I knew we could not waste time resting as we moved toward the border.

We continued to put one foot in front of the other until we heard someone at the front of the group say, "We are here. We have reached freedom. The ground of Thailand is under our feet." Aloud I said, "Thank you Lord," as I walked those last few steps.

There was not enough energy in my body to show the emotion I felt. I wanted to jump up and down. I wanted to shout, sing, and praise Jesus, but all I could do was hold my aunt up as we followed the rest of our group. I was in a daze, but as we walked, I thought about my parents and the rest of my precious family who had died in the forest. I wondered what would have happened if they had lived until this time. I missed them deeply but, without understanding all of my feelings, accepted their deaths and said, *Thank you, God, for the wonderful*

154

years I had with my parents and brothers and sisters. I also thank you for each day of freedom we will have in this new country.

These thoughts were suddenly interrupted when a man grabbed my aunt away from me and started to search her body. For a moment I thought he must be crazy. Surely he couldn't think we had anything of value. We looked like a very sick, tired group of poor people. Just then another came at me and put his hand in my clothing and around my body. I couldn't understand his words but was trying to fight and scream. He was much stronger than I, though, and there was nothing I could do. Finally, he decided I did not have any gold, so he pushed me away.

This happened to most of the people in our group. My uncle's little bit of gold was taken from him. Nan had also been carrying some, which was brutally taken from her. Later we learned these men were bandits from Thailand.

9

Refugees Seeking Refuge

Nonetheless, when I saw someone who looked to me as though he were the President of the United States, though I heard he was from the embassy in Bangkok — I went to him and tried to tell him my problem. I used a little bit of English as we talked, because I was determined to get us out of the camp. I knew that we could not physically survive many more days of living there. After talking with him, I went back to the family, filled with hope. Excitedly, I told them, "I believe God is going to get us out of this place. I pray it is soon."

. . . Finally it happened! After one month in the camp we heard the news that Nan and I were . . . going to America.

My hand shook with excitement as I put my name by Nan's on the registry in the transit camp. Underneath, I wrote in Khmer, "I worked for World Vision International in Phnom Penh." It was May 1979.

Nong Chan wasn't a real camp. The living conditions were actually worse than our village life as prisoners of war under the Khmer Rouge. This place was just a clearing with a large group of people who had nothing to do but sit and hope to be taken to a camp that was a processing center. This was just an extension, I learned quickly, of the hell-like atmosphere of our life in the forest, but we were thankful to be outside Cambodia. I didn't think we would have to be worried about being beaten or tortured, although death was still a strong possibility.

Somehow my uncle bought a large piece of plastic at a little market run by the Thai people. With a stick in the middle and on the sides to hold the plastic up, we made a tent. "It isn't very sturdy," my uncle said, "but I hope it will keep the rain off us."

Because the ground was very muddy, we had to find pieces of wood to lie on inside the tent. I was especially worried about my aunt and uncle, who had both developed bad fevers while we walked from Battambang City. Four years of living in the forest had taught me that being constantly cold and wet could mean death for one with a fever.

That first night in Nong Chan was much like the next

157

nine—rainy, windy, and cold. When the wind was strong, it blew away the sides of the plastic, and the rain swept into our "tent." One of us would then get up and put the rocks back on the edges of the plastic, but they would only roll off when the wind came again. Trying to keep the sick ones warm and dry, the rest of us slept on the edges of the tent, closest to the rain and wind. No one slept for more than a few minutes at a time, though.

We all had bad headaches, were dizzy, and nauseated from lack of food and sleep. There was no medicine available, no one was there to run this camp, so there was nowhere to go for any kind of help. There was nothing for us to do during the daylight hours but sit in the tent listening to the rain while we tried to forget our hunger and wait for the night to come.

Everywhere we walked, the ground was muddy. There was not a place to wash ourselves. There were no toilet facilities other than a wide tree. Modesty was a luxury we did not have again.

I felt so sad every time I looked at my newfound family. If it weren't for my persistence, they would not be suffering this terrible experience. "I wish we could start over," I told my uncle. "I would not encourage you to take this trip." He told me not to worry about it.

On the sixth day in Nong Chan came a wonderful rumor. "Some people from the U.S. Embassy are coming to the camp today. Perhaps some of us will be able to leave." A spark of hope! Since arriving, I had been trying to remember my English, but I was so weak physically that it was hard to concentrate and the words came to my memory very slowly. I couldn't put sentences together, and it was impossible for me to remember the names of World Vision personnel I had known in Phnom Penh.

Nonetheless, when I saw someone who looked to me as though he were the President of the United States, though I heard he was from the embassy in Bangkok—I went to him and tried to tell him my problem. I used a little bit of English as we talked, because I was determined to get us out of the camp. I knew that we could not physically survive many more days of living there. After talking with him, I went back to the family filled with hope. Excitedly, I told them, "I believe God is going to get us out of this place. I pray it is soon."

On our tenth day in the camp the embassy officials returned in a large bus. Everyone was excited to see them, and we could hardly wait to find out what they were going to do. They told us, "We have been in Bangkok and checked through the names of the people registered in Nong Chan. We cannot take you all away from here now, but those people who hear their names should get on the bus to go to Lumpini Camp near Bangkok." That was the place we had all heard about and been hoping for—a big step on the road to freedom!

One of the men began to read names. As he read, I listened. I was afraid I wouldn't hear our names. On the other hand, I was afraid that if I didn't listen he would say them and I would never know it. Suddenly in the middle of those thoughts, I very clearly heard him say, "Ly Nan; Ly Lorn." He had called our names!

I looked at Nan to see if she had heard it, too. Her eyes were as big and surprised as mine felt, and we both realized that we could actually leave Nong Chan. Everything was so rushed and disorganized that it was only as we began to board the embassy bus that I realized the names of my aunt, uncle, and the rest of the family had not been called.

I turned around and ran back to them. It was so hard to look in my uncle's sweet face—I loved him so much and wanted them all to come with me. My heart ached as I heard him say, "Don't worry. They take a new group of people out every few days. We'll see you at the camp." With that assurance, he hugged me and turned me around to walk me toward the bus.

I didn't want to leave them in that place. As I said goodbye, tears were streaming down my face and there was a prayer in my heart that these dear people would be able to come to the Lumpini Camp also. They were my family, my security. There was nothing more I could do. We still had no control over our lives. We had to do what we were told to do. Nothing else was possible.

I had guilt feelings as we drove past all the people whose names had not been called. My uncle's family was only fourteen of hundreds who stood there forlornly watching us leave them behind, but the faces of my family stood out in the crowd and the look on my uncle's face seemed to say, "Don't worry about us. I understand and I love you!"

The Thai soldiers on the bus talked to us. One of them tried to discourage me by saying, "The Americans will not treat you well. They will take you to a bad place and might even send you back to Cambodia." Still uncertain about whom we could trust, I momentarily wavered when he said that. But the Americans had been my friends in Phnom Penh and I would not let this soldier I didn't know convince me that good people like that would turn their backs on me now. Finally he realized I wasn't listening to him, and he went off to talk to someone else. Nan and I spent the rest of the time in almost complete silence, watching the scenery from the bus.

About 7:00 P.M. we arrived at Lumpini Camp. From the first, I felt confident about the freedom and happiness I had prayed for. I knew that God was giving it to us. For the first time in four years I saw the faces of people I had known in Phnom Penh. Alice Compain, a friend of my Bible-English teacher, Ruth Patterson, was there. She told me that Andrew Wey, a man who had gone to our church, was also working in the camp. I was dizzy with happiness. Alice held me close. She seemed to understand that I was not ready to talk about my experiences. I felt weak but joyful. Finally, after four terror-filled years, we had reached our goal of freedom.

We were taken into a large building where we would sleep. It was like a big shed with long rows of beds. There were no dividers between the beds, but I noticed right away that each one had a sheet—and a pillow! We had not seen either one in four years. There was electricity in the building and even a private place to go to the bathroom. I remember telling Nan, "Perhaps we'll never have to carry water again." Everything was so wonderful to us. Life was much better than I had remembered it could be. When we finally lay down in our beds to sleep, thoughts of our family in Nong Chan could no longer be put aside. I desperately wished I could share this with them.

The first thing I wanted to do the next morning was to wash myself. A lady showed us to a large room. "Here is where you can take showers," she told us. But first we needed to buy some things. With a little bit of gold that one of my cousins had given me as we hurriedly left for

Lumpini, I bought toothbrushes, soap, and a comb. I silently thanked her for it again. I wondered how she had been able to hide it from the Thai bandits. "We will have to use the same soap to wash our hair as we use to wash our bodies," I told Nan, "but at least we will feel clean again."

Later that day I went to find Alice Compain and told her I wanted to write a letter to Isabel, my friend with whom I had worked in the World Vision medical clinic. Alice was especially nice and she helped me express my experiences and feelings in a letter that we sent off to Isabel in Australia. It was such a privilege to talk with Alice and share the thoughts and feelings I had held inside for so long.

Even though I had plenty of good food and it had been weeks since I was forced to do the hard labor I had known for so long, I was unable to regain my strength. Alice saw how weak I looked and told me to go to the American nurse at the small clinic right away. The nurse was surprised to hear me speak to her in English. Even though I still had trouble remembering words, I enjoyed talking to her. I told her about my work in the World Vision clinic and was pleased when she said that she would like to have my help when I was strong enough.

With that incentive I had a reason to get strong again. The thought of being able to help sick people excited me. "I will be able to work again," I told Nan. "I wish Hy were here to help as he did in Phnom Penh." Several days later I went to the clinic where the nurse and I became a team. It was fun to get up in the morning. For the first time in years I felt as though I had a purpose for living. I enjoyed life. The privilege of being able to help sick people—rather than being forced to watch them die as with my own family—was wonderful.

Soon after I went to work, I learned about a Bible study held every Thursday afternoon. Another thing to be excited about! I had missed my New Testament since it was stolen in 1978. At the Bible study I was given a copy of the entire Bible, and I was free to study it and talk about it whenever I wanted. Every Sunday morning we had a worship service that was truly a sacred, beautiful time as we sat under the open sky to bow before God with both our hearts and our bodies. Everyone there had suffered in every way possible. We understood pain and loneliness. Even though we had been deeply hurt by the problems of life, we were all confident that our dear heavenly Father was stronger. We knew that we had the answer to the despair all around us! In those days I realized it would never again be enough to only thank Him with words: I had to thank Him with every day of my life.

Lumpini was filled with experiences—some of them completely new and others like new because our memories were so far in the past. We practiced using a knife, fork, and spoon. The proper use of the toilets was explained. (Some people had been using them to wash clothes!) The Western way of taking a bath was also new. The Cambodian lifestyle of bathing was to ladle (cold) water over their bodies from a bucket. We were given a tour of the camp kitchen and shown some of the Western ways of cooking. Many of our country people had never seen food in a can and would not have known how to open one. The more we were told, the more frightening everything seemed. I wondered how Nan and I would be able to cope in a foreign world by ourselves.

Thursday evening was the most fun time of the week. That was when an employee of World Vision in Bangkok, Paul Jones, visited the camp. He had an infectious smile that made everyone happy. I liked Paul from the first time I saw him—a great surprise for me.

I had only been in the Lumpini Camp for three days when I heard my name called over the loudspeaker system, "Ly Lorn. Please come to the main building. Ly Lorn." They repeated that several times before I finally went. I was afraid—afraid they would send me back to Nong Chan or even to Cambodia. Finally I gathered the courage to go and admit that I was Ly Lorn.

When I arrived at the main building, I was told, "An American man is waiting to see you." Suddenly there he was. A big, strong man with a friendly face and eyes that told me I could trust him. From that moment I knew he would help me. Paul Jones did help me—and many others like me.

Every Thursday night Paul and I had a great time distributing the things he brought to the camp. There were vitamins, special medicines, orange juice, soap, and clothing. It was such fun to help him. I especially enjoyed watching Paul when the children gathered around him. They were drawn to him electrically as if he were a magnet. He loved them, and they instantly knew it. The days were happy and I was content.

I didn't see any reason to leave Lumpini—everything I needed was in that camp except my family. I checked every day to see if they had been admitted to Lumpini and was disappointed each time. I thought about them constantly, wondering how they were feeling and if they had been transferred to a different camp.

After we had been in Lumpini for about two weeks, on June 5 my happy, beautiful world fell apart. I heard the bad news that our bus had been the last to leave Nong Chan. All of the people left—including my aunt, uncle, and their family—had been pushed back into Cambodia by the Thai government. They had come so close to freedom and happiness, then it was all taken from them—and they were forever taken from me. I became very depressed.

Someone tried to explain: "It is because Thailand has very difficult political problems and has been forced to return some of the refugees to Cambodia. The people have been taken to a safe area." I knew this simply meant that no active fighting was going on. I also knew that nothing along the border was "safe" because that was where the Pol Pot troops were hiding. I had walked there and I knew what it was like.

After talking to many people, I learned that the Khmer Rouge had set many land mines to kill those who left the narrow trail on which the people who were sent back were to walk. The trail was both steep and muddy, so many died that way. Anyone who tried to turn back and escape was immediately shot. With only the two-day food supply given them by the Thais, I knew the rest would have starved. I cried when I thought of how sick my aunt and uncle had been when I left for Lumpini. I remembered their children and became angry that they had had to go through that terrible experience. And I felt guilty that I had freedom. How could I live with myself?

My guilt was as deep as my anger and depression. "If

I hadn't encouraged my uncle and his family, they would never have left the safety of their little home in Battambang City. It was their gold that had bought our tickets to freedom, and I cannot understand why Nan and I made it and they did not," I tearfully told Alice.

Nan and I were registered with the Lutheran Welfare Committee, and Paul Jones asked the people at World Vision in the United States if they could help us find a sponsor. There were many papers to fill out and forms to sign, but finally Paul told me, "You have a sponsor and can go to the United States when your passports are complete."

It wasn't possible for us to go to Bangkok to buy some clothes to wear on the airplane until our passports were ready, so Paul Jones sent a tailor to the camp to measure Nan and me. Then he would be able to make some clothes for us. After the tailor left, I began to get excited. "We will again have something nice to wear, something besides black," I told Nan. I remembered the times in the forest when I didn't think I'd ever again wear nice clothes or feel like a young girl, but knew I was truly blessed to have the privilege once more.

The activities around the camp, the good food and vitamins in my body, new friends around me, and the great hope of a wonderful life in America worked together to bring a new joy to my personality that I had not felt for years. It was so good to be happy again.

One day we learned that our passports were complete. We could take a bus into Bangkok to shop before leaving on our trip to America, so we were given a little money and went to the city.

It was frightening to be in Bangkok. We did not go far from the bus because we did not want to get lost. I had forgotten how exciting and busy a city could be. Battambang City had seemed large, but I didn't think there was any end to Bangkok. "People and cars are everywhere," Nan said. "All of these people can do whatever they want." It was still hard for us to remember how freedom really felt.

I enjoyed being in the city but was glad I was not alone there. Nan and I went into a few shops and bought shoes and some small bags we could use to carry our clothing in on the airplane. When it was time to get on the bus to go back to the camp, it felt good. We knew what to do there.

Finally it happened! After one month in the camp we heard the news that Nan and I were to leave Lumpini and Thailand the *next* day. We were going to America. I had not dared to count on this really happening and was overwhelmed to know that in just a few hours I would begin the first of a whole new set of experiences. I knew that these would be far more positive than the ones I had faced in recent years.

I'll never forget that night of June 17, 1979. We did not sleep. Friends from all parts of the camp were in and out of our building all night long. One woman said, "We are all excited that you can go to America, but we're very sad to see you leave." I felt the same way. Part of me wanted to go and part of me wanted to stay and help my people in the camp. I was glad when it was 4:00 A.M.—time for us to board the bus for the Bangkok airport. Through tears I waved goodbye.

I was excited. I was on my way to America, "the land of the free!"

10

I Feel Like a Child Again

It didn't take us long to get ready, but just in case we didn't soon get the chance again, we each took another hot bath. Everything about America was so new and wonderful to us — the comforts so unbelievable that I was sure this must be something like heaven.

As Nan and I rode the bus to the airport that early June morning, my excitement was mixed with fear. My mind went back to other major moves we had made. They had been filled with hope, too. I wondered if it was possible that we would be disappointed and hurt again.

I thought of the time we had ridden the motorbikes from Ang Tasaom to Phnom Penh. I was sixteen and filled with optimism then. I had never been sad before. The years in Phnom Penh were good, so I was still optimistic, though more frightened, when I was twenty-one and we were forced to evacuate our home and walk to Mother's birthplace in Takeo in 1975. That was a devastating experience as we tried to learn to be farm people.

We were sure the answer to our future had come when we were told that the leader of the Khmer Rouge regime, Pol Pot, wanted all of the city people to join him in Battambang Province. After four months of hard living conditions in Takeo, the promise of a comfortable life was wonderful, so I was optimistic about our move until we were on our way to Battambang. The experiences of that truck ride made me realize that we were being governed by a very evil man and there was nothing we could do to change it.

Finally, after four heart-breaking years in the forest of Battambang Province, we had taken another journey—a happy one that led us to relatives of our parents in Battambang City. After a few weeks of living with our newfound family, the promise of freedom together prompted us to escape from Cambodia and go to the Nong Chan camp on the Cambodia-Thailand border—a sad experience. Sad because I lost another family. God granted freedom to my sister and me when we were allowed to go to the Lumpini Camp near Bangkok.

* * *

Sitting next to Nan on the bus as we rode to the airport, I cried. I was sad and happy, frightened and excited. I hoped and prayed that the move from Bangkok to Los Angeles, California, would be our last. I could not be sure, though, and I was afraid to hope— there had been so many disappointments!

As I sat there, I felt a sense of peace come over me and I began to remember the things that had happened to make the trip possible. I decided that our future in America was planned by God and was His reason for bringing us through the dark days in the forest and our trip to the Thai border. I knew—all of a sudden I confidently knew!—that God was going to use and bless us in America.

We rode for about an hour on the bus before arriving at the Bangkok airport. Then we began the long process of filling out papers and showing them to different people as they checked and rechecked us. When everything was completed, we still had to wait several hours before boarding the plane, but we enjoyed watching the people go by us.

As we waited, we chatted together with the other refugees around us. People were saying, "Everyone here is in such a hurry. I wonder where they could all be going." Others wondered about our approaching flight with questions like, "What will it feel like to fly? Will we be able to eat on the plane? Will there be a place to go to the bathroom?" And the question most often asked was, "Will there be someone to meet our flight? Do you think they want us in their country or will they resent us?"

Nan and I had only been outside Cambodia for about six weeks, so our bodies were still very weak. This new adventure was quite a shock to us, but I continued to trust God, remembering, "I will never leave thee nor forsake thee." I felt sure that "even in Los Angeles, California" could be added!

When they called for us to get on the plane, Nan and I were anxious. We were ready to take the risk, even though our fear of loneliness and the many unknowns was great. Really, we knew we had no choice.

The airline stewardesses were very nice and worked hard to make us feel comfortable. Soon we were in the air, and I realized that flying didn't hurt at all. We were given several different meals, but they usually had to wake me to eat. Nan and I both slept most of the trip, and I was surprised to hear the pilot's voice saying, "Good morning everyone. We will land in Los Angeles, California in one hour. It is a nice, warm evening and you can already see the lights of the city in the distance." It was morning for us, but it was evening here. I hadn't realized that would be true.

I tingled with excitement and couldn't resist giving Nan a big hug. She was still half asleep, so this surprised her, but she was accustomed to my impulsiveness and listened as I talked about the "exciting life God is going to give us in California." I loved to daydream and told her, "I just know, Nan, that we are going to meet many people in America who will love us and let us be part of their families. I believe God will help us learn the language well so that we can get jobs and be like other Americans. Oh, Nan, you will love them so much," I promised. (Nan had not worked at the World Vision clinic so had not had opportunities to know any Americans.) I was anxious to have her meet the loving, generous type of people I had come to know so well in Phnom Penh.

It was June 18, 1979—four years and two months since we had been forced to leave Phnom Penh as a family of eleven people. Now Nan and I were a family of two and ready to begin life in America.

Because the flight arrived late, some of the people from the Lutheran Welfare Committee met our plane and took us to a hotel near the airport. They told us, "Someone from World Vision will come to pick you up in the morning." The heavy emotional strain of the "newness" of everything had made us very tired, so we were looking forward to a good sleep. Tomorrow we would begin meeting new friends.

In Lumpini they had told us about the American bathtubs, and we were anxious to experiment with one. At first we had trouble regulating the temperature of the water, but soon it was just right and we each enjoyed a long, hot bath. The bath towels were large and so nice and white—the bed sheets soft and clean, the pillows big and fluffy. Having running water that was nice and warm—and a room so beautiful—almost made me burst with happiness and excitement. I went from one part of the room to another. I pushed a button that turned on a television set. Even though we had had one in Phnom

Penh, I now marveled at the miracle of it. I picked up the telephone and heard a woman's voice at the other end. Mumbling an "I'm sorry," I quickly put the receiver down.

Everything was so new and wonderful that I had trouble settling down. Seeing Nan almost asleep in the big soft bed, I realized that I, too, was tired. Reluctantly I went to bed, leaving one light on for a bit of security.

We hadn't even thought about how we would know when it was time to meet the person from World Vision and were surprised and a little frightened to hear a knock on the door about 10:00 the next morning. "A man—a Mr. George Hahn—is waiting for you in the lobby," we were told.

It didn't take us long to get ready, but just in case we didn't soon get the chance again, we each took another hot bath. Everything about America was so new and wonderful to us—the comforts so unbelievable that I was sure this must be something like heaven. We were a little afraid to meet an American man because we didn't know what to say to him. I wondered if our clothes were "right" and where he was taking us—my mind was filled with a million questions as we pressed the button for that strange new thing called an elevator.

As we walked into the lobby, I didn't know how we would find him, but Mr. Hahn knew us right away. Looking around at other people, all wearing Western-style clothing, I realized immediately that we must look like poor country girls. I felt a little embarrassed. But Mr. Hahn's kindness helped us to feel very comfortable. "You must be hungry," he said. "Let's go have some breakfast together."

I could tell that Nan was very frightened at this. We

had been taught in the camp about the use of silverware and table manners, but after four years without thinking of those things, they were difficult to remember. "Just watch what he does, Nan, and do the same thing," I said in Khmer. We quickly learned that when we needed to communicate about a problem like this, we could do it in our own language. We hoped people didn't know that we were frightened. We didn't want them to worry about us.

Mr. Hahn realized that we didn't know what to order, so he asked the waitress for orange juice, eggs, and toast for each of us. It sounded good, and I realized that I was very hungry.

Not being aware of our background or the extent of the suffering we had known in Cambodia, one of Mr. Hahn's first questions was "Where is the rest of your family?" As those words penetrated our minds, something inside each of us burst, and in the middle of that restaurant our emotions were released in a gush of tears. Poor Mr. Hahn did not know what to do as he sat there with two Cambodian girls who could hardly understand English and could not even stop the sound of their own sobs. He waited patiently, trying to quiet us with his kind words.

By the time our food arrived, we had somewhat regained our composure and were able to share with him a little of the life we had known in Cambodia. We did not tell him too much, though. It was just too personal and too soon to try to put our feelings and the stories of the deaths of our family members into words. Sensing this, Mr. Hahn began talking about other things and soon had us smiling as he told us funny stories.

Even though we didn't really understand them, it was still fun to be able to laugh again.

After breakfast we drove across the city of Los Angeles to Monrovia—the city where the World Vision offices are located. The buildings along the way amazed us. Nan and I couldn't believe our eyes. Everything was so big, there were so many people on the streets, and the cars frightened me as they whizzed by us. "I feel like there is a movie theater all around us," I said to Nan.

Finally we arrived in Monrovia. Mr. Hahn took us to an apartment owned by World Vision, where we could stay until something more permanent was found for us. Mr. Hahn took us to a Chinese shop where we could buy some of the food that we wanted—and of course, rice. It felt so good to be able to cook our own food, eat when we were hungry, sleep as long as we wanted to, and have what seemed like total luxury all around us. The physical and emotional exhaustion was so great that we used this time to recover, sometimes sleeping for many hours at a time.

Every day Mr. Hahn came to see us. After a few days he thought we were accustomed enough to meet new people, and he invited us to see the World Vision offices, and visit with some of the people there. "I wish there were a way to tell these people how much we appreciate their love and help," Nan said to me as we were getting dressed for the occasion. We decided that the only way to thank them was by helping someone else whenever we had the chance. I hoped it would come soon.

While we were at World Vision, we met one of the secretaries, Gloria Ruiz. She was very nice to us and offered to help us any way she could. Within the next two days Gloria and her family visited us at the apartment, and I knew then that we would be very special long-time friends.

Loneliness had been the greatest fear I had faced in coming to America. I was so thankful that God was giving us a new family—His family. The most exciting part for me was when Nan became a Christian. I had known for many weeks that she wanted to take that step, but because it had to be *her* decision, I had not pressed her about it. She accepted Jesus into her life while we were staying in the World Vision apartment. When she told me, "Lorn, I have Jesus in my heart," I cried for joy. Through my tears, I said, "Now, Nan, we are sisters in every way! I am so thankful to God for this wonderful gift."

With the help of the people at World Vision we met other Cambodians. I even met some I had known in Phnom Penh. They told us that there was a group of Christians who met together every Sunday afternoon. I prayed, *Oh, dear Jesus, I want so much to go, to worship with other Cambodians. I love Americans very much, but I am lonesome to see the faces of other Cambodians, to hear them speak our language and to sing with them, but there is no way for me to get to that church. It is too far away.* The Lord responded to that desperate plea quickly, and I soon had a phone call offering us a ride to that Sunday afternoon service. It became a wonderful Sunday tradition. Those times together with people who had had experiences similar to ours helped us greatly.

Nan and I were both pleased the day that Mr. Hahn came to tell us that Gloria and her family wanted us to live in their home. We were so excited because we knew this was a wonderful chance to be part of a beautiful family and to learn to understand our new homeland.

Within a few days of our arrival in our new home, we were enrolled in English classes and had a routine for studying. My memory of English was returning, but there was still much to learn. Every morning when I opened my eyes, I was excited to get up because I knew that God had given me another day, another chance to learn, another chance to love the people around me, and most of all, another chance to live for Him without being afraid that someone might kill or torture me. What a privilege!

Because Nan had very little English background, the language was more difficult for her. She progressed well, though, and was soon communicating with the Ruiz children. They were a great help in acquainting us with life in America. Their unconditional acceptance of us made us feel at home and loved even when the painful memories of our past were the strongest. God had been so good in healing our hearts and minds. As I look back on the years we lived under the Pol Pot regime, I realize that my dear heavenly Father gave me what I needed each step of the way. I wouldn't have had the strength to survive the terror and torture combined with the loss of each loved one except for the fact that with each particular situation, His hand holding me up seemed to give a bit more strength.

Sometimes in those last five years, I had been so desperate that I felt like a child lost in a maze. Even though I was screaming, no one would help me. When I became quiet and listened for something from God, He always made Himself and His love known to me. The Pol Pot forces had managed to keep us so terror-stricken that God often seemed far away, and it was hard to ask for His help.

Now I feel like a child who has been found and is safe and secure in a new family of Christian loved ones who truly care. I feel that God has brought me through something that must be similar to hell itself, but the point is that He *has* brought me through it. Now I'm free. I have a new life, hope for the future, the opportunity to try anything I want to do. For that I can only praise God.

After living for several months with Gloria's family, Nan and I decided it was time for us to become more independent. Gloria helped us find an apartment. When our need for furniture was made known, many Christian friends, especially those from our sponsors, the Sierra Madre Congregational Church, gave us the things we needed. One man gave us four beautiful new chairs for our living room. Others gave beds, lamps, towels, sheets, dishes—all the things we could ever need. We felt so loved and so blessed to have people in our lives who wanted us to be happy in America. Every day we thank God for this wonderful country!

One of the most beautiful, meaningful days of my life was April 20, 1980—just about a year after the Vietnamese takeover of Cambodia. That was the day that Nan and I, along with twelve other Cambodians, were baptized by our Cambodian pastor, San Hay Seng. There was an almost-indescribable air of worship in the sanctuary of the church that day. So many of the people had been experiencing brutal persecution just a few months before that time that the joy of having the freedom to be part of a public declaration of faith in Jesus Christ and His great power was wonderful. I will never take that freedom for granted.

We have been in America since 1979 and continue to have new experiences. At first we were frightened about learning to shop in the supermarket, take the bus, pay bills, communicate in English—especially on the telephone, use the washing machines, and do all the other things Americans do every day. Now they've become part of our lives, too.

Nan and I were both able to get jobs, buy a car, and continue to study in our spare time. I was able to pass the exam indicating I have the equivalent of a high school diploma.

Probably the most exciting thing that could have happened to us happened the day that we learned that our aunt, uncle, and cousins (whom we had left in Nong Chan), plus an aunt we had not seen since 1974 in Phnom Penh were alive in a camp in Thailand. We had been devastated to know that they had been sent from Nong Chan back to Cambodia. I can only imagine what they must have suffered. Now we heard that they were in Thailand. That gave us a stronger-than-ever reason to hope and pray for their admittance to America. Finally, one day in April of 1981 that happened. Our joy was indescribable, but I'm sure you can understand that one day Nan and I had no family—the next day there was a large family again!

Those loved ones are now happily settled in America. Somehow, one of their daughters had escaped from Cambodia and made her way to Canada. She had been able to get a good job and was able to sponsor her whole family. So it was that they were able to come to freedom in the spring of 1981. How I thank God for that wonderful gift!

When we learned that Mother's sister and family had escaped, we thought *maybe it could happen again*: Maybe Father's sister and her family could have escaped—maybe we even had other relatives still alive whom we didn't know about!

So Nan and I put our photographs in the Chinese paper in Thailand. Then we prayed that if we had relatives in any of the Thai camps, they would see the photos and write to us.

Well, it worked! My father's sister and her family were in a refugee camp when they saw our photos and wrote to us. Then we began the long process of filling out forms and answering questions so that we could get permission to bring these loved ones to America.

Finally we were granted the right to sponsor the whole family. It was a thrill to welcome them to our new country and our home. It was a bit crowded, but we made room for them because they were family. As we helped them adjust to this new life, we remembered how strange it had seemed to us. What a thrill to share what we had with these we loved so much.

They adjusted quickly, and soon life had become a comfortable routine for us all. They had to learn the same kinds of things Nan and I had learned—and we had the wonderful privilege of helping them.

One day my aunt told me that she and my uncle had a friend who knew a very nice man who lived in Mineral Wells, Texas. His name was Hak Y Leav. My aunt's friend had told Hak Y about me. According to our Cambodian custom, he told his sister that he would like to meet me. His sister talked to my uncle about it; my uncle told my aunt to discuss it with me.

My aunt came to me, to tell me about Hak Y. Until this time I had not even known his name. As she talked, I realized that this was the answer to one of my prayers. For years I had had a fear about the responsibility of choosing my own husband. Now my family was helping me do that.

She said, "What do you think? Would you like to meet him?" I responded by asking her opinion. She said, "He's a good man. He has a job and would give you security." So it was that Hak Y came to California to see us. Because of his job responsibilities, he was only able to stay for the weekend.

Again I talked with my aunt. "He seems very kind and gentle," she said. "I believe your father and mother would have liked him." That was really all I needed to hear. So it was that Hak Y and I became engaged.

I did not love him. In fact, I hardly knew him, but I felt some pity for him. I thought, *He's all alone. He seems nice; my family likes him. I will marry him and make a home with him.*

During the next three months Hak Y and I talked often on the telephone. Then he returned one week before our wedding. During that week we spent time getting to know each other as we had blood tests, got our marriage license, and went to family dinners. I still didn't feel love for this man, but on March 13, 1982, I became Mrs. Hak Y Leav.

According to tradition, we spent the first three nights of our married life in the small home of my aunt and uncle. There were family members and friends around the whole time. As the bride, I had to be sure that everyone was well cared for. If someone was sitting alone on the sofa, I would go talk with him to see if there was anything I could do for him. Hak Y and I had almost no time to be alone. During those days I thought often of my parents. I hoped that they would be happy and pleased with the way I was living my life.

On the fourth day, we went to Texas and the home of Hak Y's sister. Another part of our tradition is to go to the home of the groom's family after three nights in the bride's home, but we stayed longer than usual. Because we had very little money, we lived with my sister-in-law. She had four young children, and, since I didn't have a job, I was the one who stayed home with her children while everyone else went away to work. I did all the housework and cared for the children for one year.

Our first baby, Ly Houng Leav, was born on March 8, 1983. After two months, I decided that we needed a home of our own, so we moved and I went to work. It was very difficult to leave my little one, but Hak Y was good about helping to care for her. We were able to work in shifts so that she was only under someone else's care about an hour each day. As I watched my husband caring for Houng, I began to realize that my love for Hak Y had grown strong. God had given me a very special gift in my husband.

Our next three children were born in 1985, 1987, and 1989. Each time, I worked up until the birth and then took two months off work to have that special time with my new little loved one. Each child has a special personality that Hak Y and I could see beginning to develop from birth.

I don't know what will happen in the years ahead, but

from reading my story you know that I have every reason to believe and trust God to give me all I need. I may not always have all I wish for, but I will have all I need.

*   *   *

The years between April 1975 and May 1979 were very sad ones. I will never stop missing or loving my family. There isn't a day that goes by without thoughts of them. Often there are tears and sometimes an almost-overwhelming sadness. But always, God is there. I know His promise that He will never leave me is true, and it's on that I will always depend. It's that promise that helped me survive through the most difficult years of my life. And it's that promise that gives me the security I need.

ក្រុ សារ

11

Dreams for the Future

Families are very important to my people, and our children are the most important part of our lives. . . . It is very important to me that my children always stay very close and protective of each other. . . . Remembering how it was my faith that helped me survive the years under the Khmer Rouge, I want my children to have a strong faith as well.

Now I'm happy. I have security again. My husband, Hak Y Leav, is a good man. He is a welder and has had the same job for more than ten years. We have four children. We wanted a large family because we both have lost our parents and most of our family members. Families are very important to my people, and our children are the most important part of our lives.

Ly Lorn today, with her husband Hak Y and their children today

They're beautiful children. Ly Houng Leav (we call her Houng) was our firstborn. She is now seven years old. She loves going to school, and I'm very proud that she can read. She often reads to me from her school books and Sunday school papers. She is also very good at helping with the other children. She learned long ago how to help with feeding the babies, changing their diapers, and other chores that make it possible for me to have four young children. Houng wants more than anything else to be a doctor. I think she will do it.

Hak Lee Leav is five years old. He is very special to me, and often reminds me of my little brothers, who died during the years we lived under Pol Pot, the leader of the Khmer Rouge. Lee is a very special child. He loves to be cuddled, but I know that won't last for long. He enjoys preschool and makes friends easily. Sometimes, like his sister, he wants to become a doctor. Other times he wants to be a policeman. He likes the fact that they are big and strong, and protect people. I want him to be happy and able to make enough money to be secure.

Ly Chiu Leav is a precious, delightful little girl. Chiu loves to explore everything around her. People are drawn to her sweet, gentle personality. I don't know what direction she will want her life to take, but I am very sure that she will follow Houng and Lee's example. It is very important to me that my children always stay very close and protective of each other.

Ly Pheng Leav is my baby. She is one year old now, so won't really be a baby for long. In fact, her personality is already developing. She loves her big brother and sisters so much and finds great delight in following them around the house, often teasing them. Because she's the baby, she usually gets away with this, but sometimes she hides a book or toy from the others. When accused, she says she doesn't have it. Sure that she is guilty, Lee is always quick to remind her that "Jesus doesn't lie. Jesus doesn't want us to lie."

Each of the girls has *Ly*, my family name, as part of their full name. Lee has *Hak*, my husband's first name, as part of his full name. We believe this will help our children to always remember the history of their family.

We're very fortunate to have a good life. Hak Y works from 7:00 A.M. till 3:30 in the afternoon. He is good at his work and is a wonderful father. I thank God for a good husband. When he returns from work, I leave for my job in a factory. It is less than ten minutes from my house, so I can be there quickly. I work until 12:00 at night, so miss being with my family in the evenings. I've had the same job in an electronic parts factory since I began working in 1983. I work on an assembly line, and I am happy that I can work to help give my children a good, secure life.

We live in a duplex. It's small, but we have two bedrooms, a living room, and a kitchen. The children like to play outside, and we sometimes walk to a small park. Often it's too hot, and I have housework to do, so they spend much of the time playing in the house. They like to play games together. Sometimes it's school, and Houng is the teacher. Other times they play store, and Lee is the owner. I like to see my children enjoying and learning from each other. I'm very happy to be the mother of four children. It's enough for my life.

My goal in life is to take good care of my children. I want them to have the kind of home with love all around that my parents gave to me. My dream for my children is that they will always be happy and successful. I want them to go to college so they will be able to get good jobs and build secure lives. Hak Y and I set the example of working hard. The children see every day how important it is to be good and faithful in the work you do.

We sometimes say, "Your work is to study hard and get a good education. We were not able to do that, so we must work very hard and long hours for a little bit of money. You can do better than this." Houng and Lee tell me that when they grow up, they want to take care of me so that I won't have to work any more. They are good children. The only dream I can see for my husband and me is that we will be able to keep working until we see our children grown and living happy, secure lives. Perhaps one day Hak Y and I will be able to travel. That is a nice dream, but my most important dream is for my children.

My only living sister is Nan. She lives about two hours away in Dallas, Texas, with her family. We don't get to see each other very often, but we talk on the phone about every week. If one of us has something very important happening, the calls might come every day. About once a month our whole family goes to Dallas, where there is a store that sells Chinese food not available in our small town. Sometimes we stop to see Nan after we have been shopping. It's wonderful to have a sister who cares about you. She is the one I've always known I could depend upon to encourage me and help me. Nan works on a machine for a publisher. Nan's husband is very successful. He works as a supervisor for his company and makes a good home for Nan and their two children.

Other than Nan and my husband's sister, we don't have really close friends. We are so busy with so many hours of work at the factory and taking care of the children that we do not have time for other people.

Sometimes I even get too tired to go to church. But my faith and trust in God is very important to me, and I know that when I don't go to church I feel far from God. Sometimes I have to remind myself that my values are the ones my children will take. Remembering how it was my faith that helped me survive the years under the Khmer Rouge, I want my children to have a strong faith as well.

Even when I don't go to church, the children do. They love it so much. A van from the First Baptist Church picks them up and brings them home. Houng especially enjoys this part of the week. She loves to show me how she can find verses in the Bible and read them. When I have missed church, she and Lee often come home encouraging me to go the next week by saying, "People asked about you, Mama. They wanted to know if you are okay." I do thank God for the privilege of prayer and worship.

* * *

God spared Nan and me from death in the forest for a purpose. Even when the memories of experiences in the forest hurt the most, I pray that He will use our years of suffering to help others understand the importance of enjoying life, helping each other, living each day to its fullest advantage in order to bring honor to Jesus Christ. His love is powerful and works in my heart to keep me

189

from becoming bitter toward God or toward the people who caused the deaths of our loved ones.

I remember that when the men crucified Jesus as His mother watched, He said, "Father, forgive them." I believe I must do the same.

ក្តី សារ

Epilogue: Cambodia Today

Having endured the struggle for survival during the Khmer Rouge era, the Cambodian people face the challenge of rebuilding their nation, their culture, and their dignity. During the years of fighting, thousands of Cambodians sought refuge in other countries, with Thailand continuing to absorb the largest number of Cambodians. At present approximately 15,000 Cambodians live in Thailand in refugee camps, being cared for by the United Nations High Commission on Refugees (UNHCR). Another 300,000 displaced Khmer reside in border camps, cared for by the United Nations Border Relief Operation (UNBRO).

Since the withdrawal of the Vietnamese army in September 1989, the government of the People's Republic of Cambodia has been able to control the political apparatus of the country. However, at present four major factions struggle for greater political and military influence, currently grouped into two categories: The People's Republic of Cambodia (PRC), installed in 1979 by the Vietnamese government, which continues to control most of the country; and the Coalition Government of Democratic Kampuchea (CGDK), formed in 1982 due to the prompting of members of ASEAN (The Association of Souteast Asian Nations), and which is comprised of the following three factions:

The Armee Nationale Sihanoukienne (ANS), the military arm of the former Khmer leader, Prince Sihanouk, formed in 1981 to resist the Vietnamese.

The Khmer People's National Liberation Front (KPNLF), led by the elderly Son Sann. The KPNLF is a noncommunist resistance group and has the least military and political power.

The Khmer Rouge. Militarily larger than both of the other groups and led by dogmatic communistic ideology, the Khmer Rouge continue to follow many of the beliefs of their former leader, Pol Pot. In secretly located camps throughout Cambodia they conduct political training, concentrating on pleasing local groups of farmers at the village level. Across the Thai border from their sanctuaries within Cambodia, the Khmer Rouge continue their hit-and-run tactics and their practice of genocide and forced labor in isolated areas, which threatens to seriously undermine the stability and legitimacy of the government. The major impact of this war effort is felt most acutely in the northwestern regions, although the constant threat of war causes extensive upheaval and unrest throughout the entire country.

Nevertheless, hopeful trends appear in Cambodia today, contributing to a climate of great optimism about the future, which is more than just being dreamed about: The idea that all things foreign should be eradicated is no longer being adhered to as in the past; there is a willingness of the people to talk to strangers; the international aid community, who used to be housed in two hotels in town until a few months ago, are now free to live anywhere in the city; renovated houses are now being used as offices for new businesses and international organizations; telephones with international long distance dialing, telexes, and fax machines are being installed every month; and, as the economy and the political arena open, Cambodia is beginning to enjoy a greater sense of religious freedom. At the national level, policies toward Christian groups have taken a definite open stand.

Bryan Truman
Consultant to World Vision